OUTDOOR
HOME REPAIRS
MADE EASY

Other
Home Environment HELP Books
from Butterick include:

INDOOR HOME REPAIRS MADE EASY

PLAN AND BUILD MORE STORAGE SPACE

HOW TO CUT HEATING AND COOLING COSTS

FIXING FURNITURE

ELECTRICAL REPAIRS MADE EASY

PLUMBING WITHOUT A PLUMBER

SOLAR ENERGY: HOW TO MAKE IT WORK FOR YOU

OUTDOOR
HOME REPAIRS
MADE EASY

by Peter Jones

Butterick Publishing

Book Design by *Jos. Trautwein*

Illustrations by *Albert Pfeiffer, Jr.*

Library of Congress Cataloging in Publication Data

Jones, Peter, 1934–
    Outdoor home repairs made easy.

(Home environment HELP book from Butterick)
    Includes index.
    1. Dwellings—Maintenance and repair—Amateurs'
manuals. I. Title. II. Series.
TH4819.3.J67   643'.7   79–28512
ISBN 0-88421-093-6

Copyright © 1980 by
Butterick Publishing
708 Third Avenue
New York, New York 10017
A Division of American Can Company

Manufactured and printed in the United States of America.
Published simultaneously in the USA and Canada.

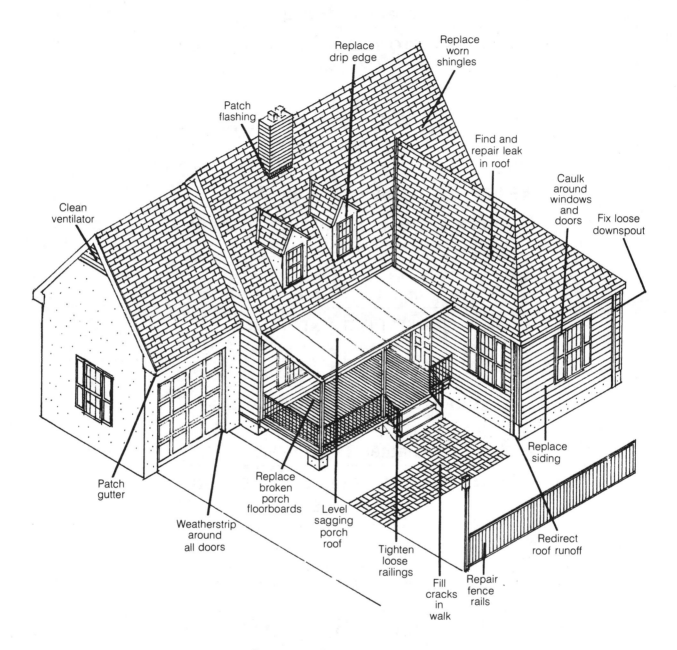

Common outdoor home repairs

chapter 1

TENDING TO THE OUTSIDE OF YOUR HOME

YOUR HOME DEMANDS a considerable amount of labor to keep it in good running order, and the indoor repairs that arise always seem to take precedence, usually because when something becomes defective inside your house it affects your day-to-day living, and is therefore more noticeable. Doors that will not close, windows that will not open, squeaky stairs, leaky faucets, lights that stop working, all become petty annoyances that sooner or later drive you to do something about them. Not so with the exterior problems.

If a little water trickles into the chimney through a crack in the mortar, you may not even notice. If there are hairline cracks in your blacktopped driveway, they have been there for years and you can still use the drive, so why bother with them? If moisture works its way under the paint below the eaves of your roof, so what? The paint peels in a small area, but nobody sees it anyway. Unless the leak in your roof works its way down to stain the top floor ceilings, you may not even be aware that there is a leak—or, that going unattended for several years, it grows dangerously worse by the season. And okay, so you can feel tiny drafts of cold air around the windows every winter, and you know that they are costing you a little extra for fuel. But the cold air is disturbing only six months of the year, and at a time when the weather is too miserable for you to do anything about it anyway.

Think of your house as an upside-down boat. There it is floating in a sea of rain and snow and parching sun and wind, all of which abrade its sides and roof in a relentless beating that sooner or later will break through its exterior skins. True, the house will not sink if it develops a leak the way a boat would, but given enough time the elements can wear away at any house until it crumbles. Rain and snow begin to rot away its timbers, dampness settles in the fibers of the wood then freezes and expands; eventually the minute crack in a basement wall becomes a crumbling hole. And so it goes, endlessly. Nature never stops working against your home, and if you don't work just as hard to keep it water- and air-tight it will, indeed, come down around your ears.

And so, into every homeowner's life there come external repairs that must be done. It is probably easiest to dedicate one weekend in the spring and another in the fall solely to exterior repairs; weekends in which you purposely go outside and *look* for things that need to be done. These repairs, and how to make them, is what this book is all about. None of them are very difficult, and many of them are so pesky that it is hard to hire anyone to do them for you. At what price, for example, do you hire a carpenter or roofer to find the leak in your attic? How much is it worth to have someone come to your home and caulk the windows? It could cost well over $100 to hire a professional to do many of the things any ten-year-old can learn to handle.

So it is less expensive to do many of the exterior repairs yourself. Moreover, a well-cared-for house automatically brings a higher price on the open market. A fresh coat of paint, for example, that costs you $350 in materials and a few days of labor, can increase the sale price of your home by as much as $5,000 or $6,000.

TOOLS

The tools you will need to make all of the repairs described in the following pages are not very many, nor are they expensive. You probably already own many of them:

Claw hammer
Screwdrivers *(standard and Phillips head)*
Pliers
Chisels (for wood)
Cold chisel *(for masonry work)*
Hacksaw
Utility saw
Portable circular power saw
Saber saw
Roofing square
Carpenter's level
Prize or crowbar
Paint brushes
Block plane
Tape or folding rule
Caulking gun
Tin snips
Shingle ripper
Utility knife
Files and rasps
Electric drill
Wrenches
Clamps
Trowel *(for masonry work)*
Putty knife
Ladder

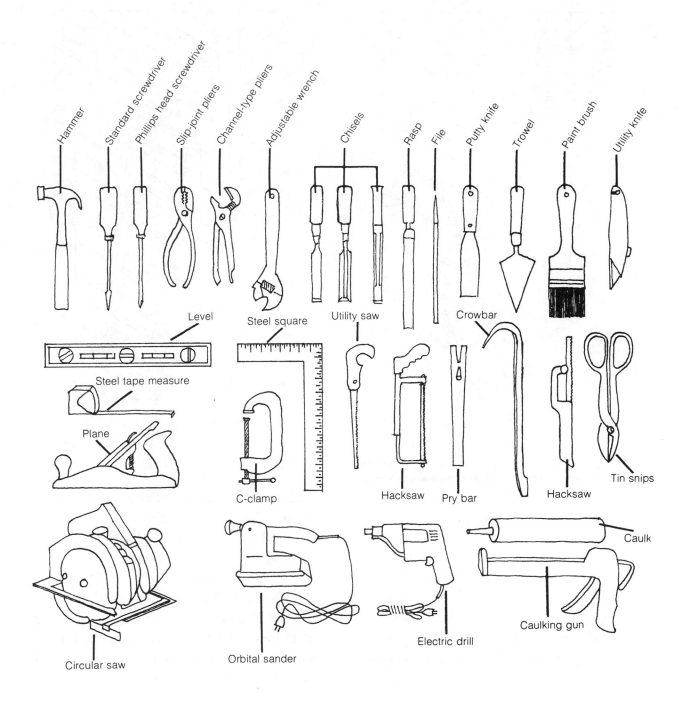

Hammer
Standard screwdriver
Phillips head screwdriver
Slip-joint pliers
Channel-type pliers
Adjustable wrench
Chisels
Rasp
File
Putty knife
Trowel
Paint brush
Utility knife

Level
Steel square
Utility saw
Crowbar

Steel tape measure

Plane

C-clamp
Hacksaw
Pry bar
Hacksaw
Tin snips

Circular saw
Orbital sander
Electric drill
Caulk
Caulking gun

Tools needed for making outdoor home repairs.

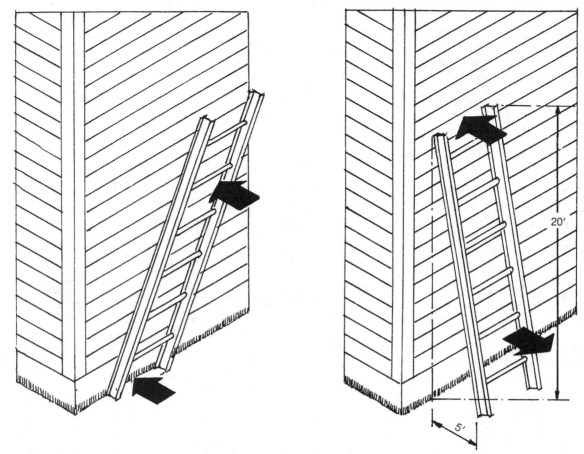

The safest way to raise and position a ladder against the side of a house.

LADDER SELECTION AND SAFETY

Perhaps the tool you'll use most often in repairing the outside of your home is a ladder. It is also one of the most frequent causes of home accidents, most of which can be avoided if you know how to choose a ladder wisely and use it safely.

Purchasing a Ladder

If you're looking to buy a new ladder, disregard price in favor of quality and strength.

Ladders are generally of three types: Type I, which will carry heavy-duty loads up to 250 pounds; Type II, a medium-duty ladder capable of carrying up to 225 pounds; and Type III, which can carry a maximum of 200 pounds and is best for light-duty and household jobs.

Test the ladder before buying, by opening it, climbing to the second rung, grasping the side rails, and trying to gently shake it to see if and how much the ladder sways. There should be no feeling of unsteadiness.

Using a Ladder Safely

Since every minute you spend on a ladder is

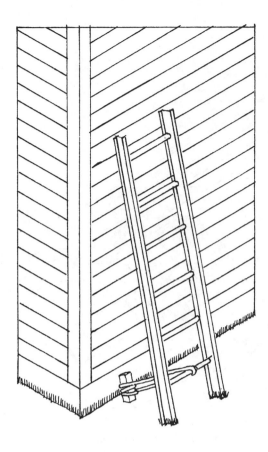

A ground-stabilized ladder.

potentially a moment of danger, follow these basic safety precautions:

• The safest way to raise a ladder is to brace its feet against the side of your house. Raise the other end over your head and walk toward the house, moving your hands from rung to rung, until it is upright. Then pull the base one quarter of the ladder's length away from the wall of the house. For example, if the ladder is 20 feet long, its base should be placed 5 feet from the wall.

• Always place the ladder so that it is level. If the ground slopes, shore up one of the feet with pieces of wood. If the ground is soft, use a wide plank under both feet.

• Jump up and down on the bottom rung of the ladder when it is in position to be sure it is solidly in place. If it is shaky, brace the bottom.

• The higher the ladder goes, the more precarious it becomes. If you are using an extension ladder and have opened it up to 20 or 30 feet, you are really taking your life in your hands when you climb up to its top rungs. You can stabilize the ladder considerably by tying its bottom rung to stakes driven in the ground. And when you get to the top, if there is any way of tying the top rung to something, do it.

• A ladder should extend at least two rungs above the highest point where you will be working. Never stand on the top two rungs of any ladder, anywhere.

• Never use a ladder in front of an unlocked door. If you are teetering atop a 20′ ladder and your kids come charging through the door and knock the ladder, you will be in a lot of trouble.

• If you have an aluminum ladder, be very careful where you place it. Aluminum is used as the conducting metal in electrical wires. *Never touch an aluminum ladder to electrical power lines;* you will find yourself standing on an uninsulated power cable.

• If you are shifting an extension ladder for

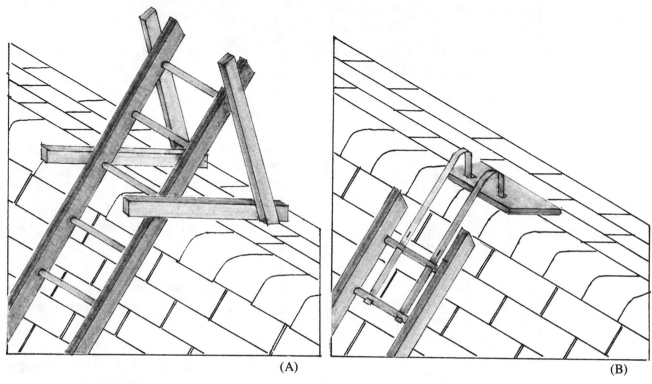

(A)   (B)

Securing a ladder to the roof with homemade supports (A) or store-bought brackets (B).

any distance, collapse it. Long ladders are ungainly objects and hard to control by yourself.

- Never place the top of a ladder against a window sash or so close to the edge of a roof that it can slide out of position. If the ladder must lean against aluminum gutters, your weight will dent the gutters unless the ladder is almost vertical. This means its base is likely to be less than the prescribed one quarter of the ladder length away from the wall. So to save the gutters and yourself, have someone brace the ladder while you are on it.

- If you are going to be working on a steep roof, you can buy brackets that will secure the ladder to the roof peak, or you can make them yourself. You can also buy ladder stabilizers to hold the top of the ladder in place against a wall, particularly if you are working atop a tall extension ladder.

- Anytime you are on a ladder, keep your hips well between its vertical rails. Extending yourself a few extra inches to get at something that is just beyond your reach is the most dangerous thing you can do on a ladder. Don't be lazy. Get down off the ladder and move it.

• If you must work with both hands while you are on a ladder, put one leg between the rungs and hook your heel back over the rung you are standing on. But have someone brace the ladder for you while you are working this way, because if the ladder falls, you can't get untangled from it fast enough to escape injury.

• For your own comfort, wear hard-soled work shoes when you must stand on a ladder for any period of time. Sneakers or soft-soled shoes will not protect your arches, and your feet will ache for days afterward.

Keep hips between vertical rails when reaching for something while on a ladder.

The safest way to stand on a ladder when both hands are busy.

chapter 2

ROOF REPAIRS

FOR ALL OF THE PROTECTION they give, roofs are remarkably simple in their construction and repair. The exterior surface of the roof may be any of several different materials, including asphalt, asbestos, wood, gravel, metal, slate, tile, or mineral-coated roofing paper. Whatever the material, it has been nailed or stapled to water-resistant roofing paper laid over a wooden sheathing, which has been nailed to the rafters attached to the top of the walls of your house. The sheathing. is most often solid sheets of plywood, between ⅛″ and ¾″ thick, but it could be made of 6″-wide tongue-and-groove boards or 6″

boards that are spaced a few inches apart. The rafters that support the roof are typically 2″ × 6″ stock that angle up to a 2″ × 8″ ridgepole, which runs the length of the roof at its highest point, or peak.

Roofing material is always applied to the roof beginning at the eaves, or the lowest edge of the roof, and each course of material overlaps the course below it. In most cases the courses are nailed to the sheathing so that the nails will be covered by the course above it. To have an exposed nailhead anywhere on a roof is to have a point where water can potentially enter your house.

Further protection against water seepage is provided by flashing. Flashing is sheet metal—usually galvanized steel, aluminum, copper—or roofing paper, nailed around the base of every chimney, skylight, dormer, vent, or pipe that protrudes through the roof, as well along any valley in the roof and often along the hips and peak. Once in place, the

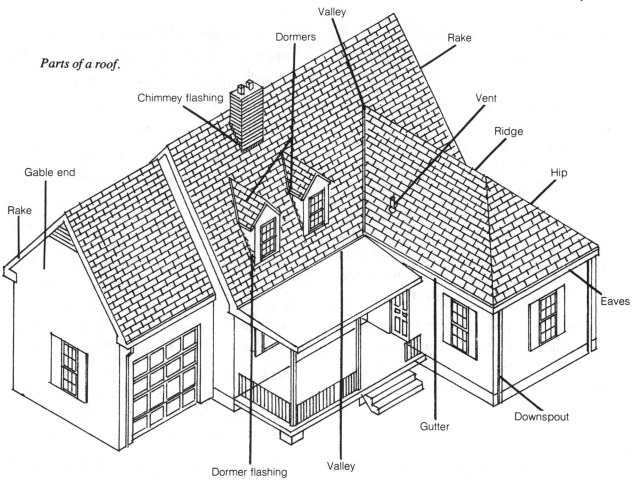

Parts of a roof.

flashing is given a protective coating of roofing cement and covered by the roofing material. Leaks, when they occur in a roof, can most often be traced to a faulty joint between the flashing and whatever projection it is protecting.

Leaks

YOUR ROOF CAN UNEXPLAINABLY develop a leak almost anytime, and for a variety of reasons:

• All houses settle, very often at a different rate than their chimneys. Hence, the flashing around the base of the chimney may pull away from the chimney or the roof.

• The caulking or roofing cement used to protect various joints and seams throughout the roof can dry out and crack, allowing water to seep under it, further loosening its bond.

• Most flashing is metal. It can corrode, rust through, become bent out of shape, all of which lessens its protection against water.

• Alternate heat and cold will cause the different materials in any roof to expand and contract at different rates. This activity pulls at sealed joints, eventually breaking them open.

• Wood rots or can be destroyed by certain fungi and insects. Wooden shingles or shakes may look quite solid, when actually they have rotted enough to allow water to seep through them.

• The wind, falling branches, heavy storms, can tear away at the roofing material, causing damage that allows water to enter your house. Here at least you will be able to see where the trouble is and repair it.

• In northern climates, ice can build up in the gutters and then back up under the first course of shingles, where it is able to seep through the sheathing and into your house.

Finding Leaks from Outside

Many leaks can be located just by walking around on the roof and carefully examining each of its parts. Do not go up on a roof when it is wet, or if the day is windy, and always wear rubber-soled shoes. Investigate the roof thoroughly, looking for the following:

• Broken shingles.

• Cracks or holes in caulking around all vent pipes and ventilators.

• Signs of rust, pinholes, or corrosion in any exposed flashing around the vent pipes and ventilators, in the valley flashing, and around the chimney bases. In particular, note whether the top edges of the flashing are secure against the metal or mortar in the chimney and that the caulking is watertight.

• Examine the joint between the flue liner and the chimney cap for cracks or breaks.

• Check the chimney cap for cracks.

• Check all flashing around skylights and each of the angles made by dormers for weak seals.

• Rock and gravel roofing, as well as roll roofing, are applied to flat roofs. Cracks, blisters, and tears can develop in the roofing paper and the tar or roofing cement used to seal the courses. The roofing paper itself can wear away, or settle into low spots where water will collect and remain in puddles.

• Look at all joints where a porch or garage roof attaches to the walls of the house. The joint should be caulked and the caulking must be in good condition.

• Check the ridge line. The peak of any roof is especially subject to wind erosion. Shingles can crack more easily here, since they are bent over the ridge to begin with. The wind can tear shingles apart or work them loose enough for water to get under them.

• Take a careful look along the eaves, just above the gutters, for any shingles that may have lifted or been damaged.

Finding Leaks from Inside

Sometimes, such as during a rain storm, it is easier to find a leak from inside the house. When water begins to damage an upstairs ceiling, you cannot assume the leak is directly

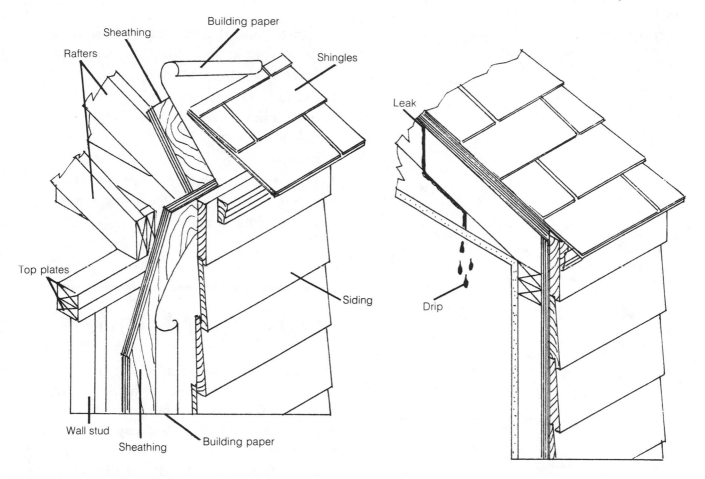

The various layers comprising the exterior of a house.

A leak in a pitched roof often originates at an angle higher than the drip.

above the damaged area. If the roof is flat, there is a fairly good chance that the leak is coming from the area directly over the damaged portion of the ceiling, but if the roof is even slightly pitched, the water may be entering at a higher point than where it drips on the ceiling. It may work its way under a shingle or deteriorated flashing and then run down the sheathing or one of the rafters for quite a distance before it drips down to the attic floor or the top floor ceiling.

The next time it rains . . .

1 • Go up to the attic with a flashlight and start your hunt from the general area above where the leak is showing itself.

2 • If there is insulation under the roof, you may have to remove the batts until you find one that is damp or discolored. When you have located the drip, track it back to its entry point.

3 • Mark the point of entry with chalk, a felt-

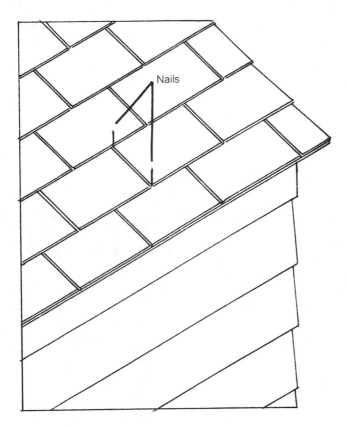

Nails

Mark a drip's point of origin by hammering nails into the sheathing from inside.

tipped marking pen, or by driving nails into the sheathing or rafters. Or, if you can see a hole, push a wire up through it so you can locate the hole from outside the roof.

4 • Select the nearest reference point that you can also use on the outside of the roof and measure the distance from the leak to that point. Good reference points to use are any vent pipe, a chimney, a corner or an end of the house, the ridgepole or the eaves.

Then, when the roof is dry and safe to walk on . . .

1 • Use the measurements you made, applying them to your reference points on the top of the roof, to locate the general area where water is entering your house.

2 • Carefully examine the entire area of the roof for any loose or broken shingles, deteriorated flashing, loose nails, or cracked caulking.

3 • When you have located the portion of the roof in disrepair, make the appropriate repairs or replacements.

Tools and Materials

THE TOOLS NEEDED TO REPAIR roofing materials are a claw hammer, shingling hatchet, putty knife, small trowel or shingle ripper, and perhaps a small crowbar. You may require an electric drill.

In addition to the shingles or tiles themselves, you will need galvanized or rust-resistant roofing nails, 1½″ to 2″ in length, and asphalt or plastic roofing cement.

The repairs made to roofing materials may be as simple as applying a thick coating of roofing cement over the damage, or may entail replacement of several shingles. It may be difficult to identify the material used to cover the roof. If you are new to the house, search your attic, cellar and garage for left-over shingles before you go out and buy a new bundle which, most likely, will not exactly match the color of your roof.

Whenever possible, work on the roof on a

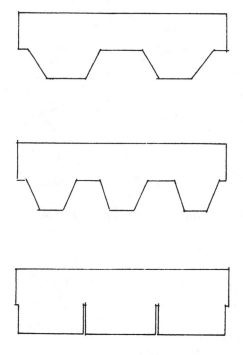

Basic forms of asphalt shingles.

warm day so that the roofing material will be more pliable and easier to handle.

Asphalt Shingles

ASPHALT SHINGLES ARE manufactured in strips and as individual shingles, and are available in a range of patterns, designs, colors, and weights. They are constructed from felt (paper) that is permeated with asphalt and then coated with mineral granules. Because they are durable, fire-resistant, and relatively inexpensive, asphalt shingles are used on practically all new construction and account for the roofing on most residences in America. They can be damaged by falling branches, severe wind or storm conditions, and must be replaced roughly every five to seven years.

Repairing Torn, Curled, or Damaged Shingles

1 • Lift the edge of the shingle.

2 • Daub the underside of the shingle with roofing cement.

3 • Press the shingle back in place.

4 • If the day is cold or windy, weight the shingle so that it stays in place. If the curl in

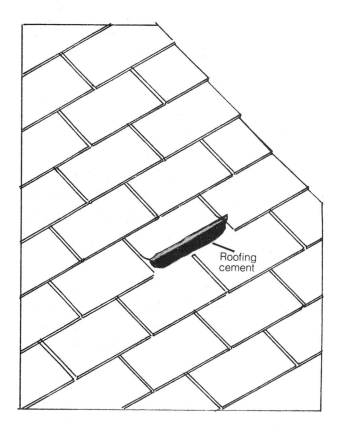

Roofing cement

A daub of roofing cement will repair a curled shingle.

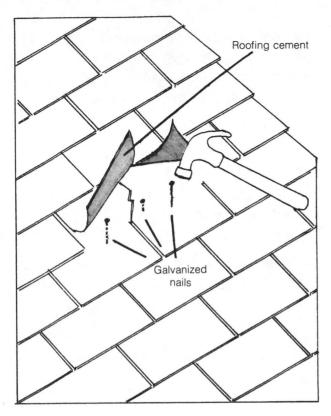

Torn shingles that resist roofing cement should be nailed.

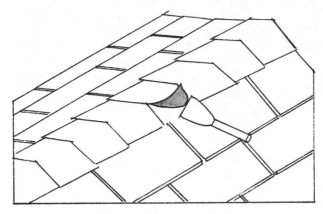

Hip shingles are apt to develop cracks, which must be filled to prevent leaks.

the shingle refuses to straighten out, or the tear pops loose, you may have to nail it. Use as few nails as possible and cover their heads with a liberal coating of roofing cement.

Repairing Hip and Ridge Shingles

Hip and ridge shingles are manufactured with a fold along their center line so they will fit over the angled hip and ridge joints of a roof. The shingles are repaired in the same way other shingles are repaired, but because they are bent they may develop cracks along the fold that will eventually become large enough to admit water. You can fill small cracks with asphalt roof paint or roofing cement.

Replacing Badly Damaged Asphalt Shingles

Badly damaged shingles should be replaced with new shingles that match the rest of the roof in style, weight, and color.

1 • Lift the edge of the shingles covering the damaged shingle. Be careful not to break the good shingles by bending them too far. (Illustration A)

2 • Remove the nails that hold the old shingle in place. You can use a prybar, crowbar, or a hammer claw to pull the nails out of the shingle. Or, if none of these tools work, insert the blade of a putty knife or flat-bladed trowel under the heads of the nails.

About 8 out of every 10 shingles can be pulled free. You may have to wiggle it slightly, taking care not to damage the shingles around it, but it can usually be yanked out of position, leaving the nails in the roof. Hammer the nails down or pull

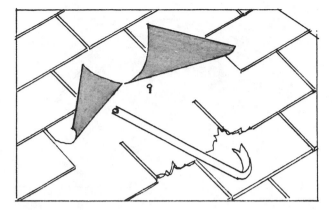

Replacing asphalt shingles. (A)

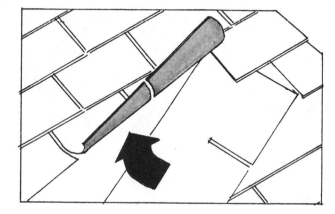

(B)

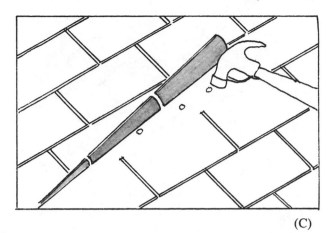

(C)

them out, whichever is easier to do without ruining the shingles you are bending back above the nails.

3 • When the old shingle is removed, slide its replacement into position. (Illustration B)

4 • Nail the new shingle to the sheathing with galvanized nails. Place three or four evenly spaced roofing nails in the new shingle, well up under the raised shingles. (Illustration C) So long as the nailheads are completely covered by the shingle above them, they need not be covered with roofing cement.

5 • Press the shingles above the new shingle back into place. If they resist lying flat again, smear a daub or two of roofing cement to their undersides and push them flat, weighting them if necessary.

Replacing Badly Damaged Hip or Ridge Shingles

1 • Lift the edge of the shingle above the damaged shingle.

2 • Pry the nails out of the damaged shingle or pull the shingle loose and hammer the nails down.

3 • Remove the damaged shingle.

4 • Hip and ridge shingles may be a preformed shingle, or they can be a half or a third of a standard shingle that has been cut and bent. Try to match the replacement shingles to the rest of the hip or ridge shingles. Paint the underside of the new shingle with roof cement and insert it in position.

5 • Hammer in a nail at each corner of the replacement shingle. (Illustration D)

6 • Apply a liberal daub of roofing cement over each nailhead. (Illustration E)

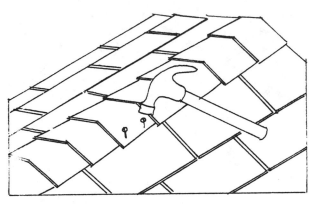

Replacing a hip shingle. (D)

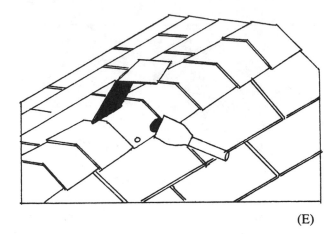

(E)

7 • Press the shingle above the replacement shingle down over the nailheads. The roofing cement will act to hold the shingle in place.

Wooden Shakes and Shingles

BOTH SHAKES AND SHINGLES are made from redwood, red cedar, or cypress, all of which have a natural high resistance to rotting and decay, but no fire resistance unless they are specially treated. The difference between a shingle and a shake is in appearance; shakes are hand split and therefore look rippled and weather-beaten; they also cost more.

Tools • Of particular use when working with wooden shingles or shakes is a shingle hatchet, which can be used to split and trim the wood as well as hammer nails. You will also need a shingle ripper for getting at the nails that hold a shingle or shake in place. You

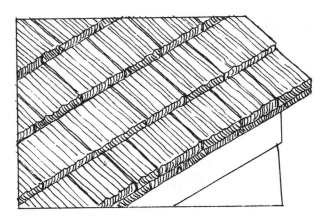

Shakes are split by hand and have a rough textured surface.

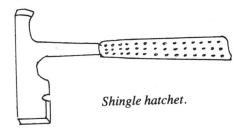

Shingle hatchet.

can buy the ripper or manufacture one from a 2′ piece of strap iron.

To make a shingle ripper: 1) Cut a notch near one end of a 2′ × 2′ iron strap. The notch must be wide enough to fit around 5d common nails. 2) Bend the unnotched end of the strap

Shingle ripper.

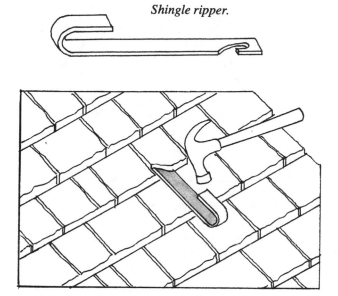

Using a shingle ripper.

into a U, to provide a hitting surface for your hammer.

To use a shingle ripper: 1) Slide the notched end of the ripper under the shake or shingle and move it around until you hook a nail in its notch. 2) Hit the bent end of the ripper with your hammer or shingling hatchet until the nail comes free.

Replacing Wooden Shingles and Shakes

When a wood shingle or shake roof develops leaks, it is usually because one or more of the shakes or shingles have become warped or split. As a rule, you cannot patch a warped or split shingle or shake. You have to replace it.

The chore of replacing wooden shakes or shingles is not particularly difficult, but you must work very carefully or you may damage the surrounding material. It should be noted that many shake or shingle roofs are not supported by a full sheathing, but are nailed to boards spaced a few inches apart, in what is known as open sheathing. It is the nature of both wooden shingles and shakes that you might be able to stand in your attic on a sunny day and look up at all manner of cracks admitting rays of sunshine. Don't be alarmed. The roof still may be watertight, particularly if it has been well laid and the individual shakes or shingles are still solid. If you should need to replace any wooden shingles or shakes, follow this procedure:

1 • Using either a shingling hatchet or a hammer and chisel, split the damaged shingle into strips. (Illustration F)

2 • Pull the strips of wood free of the roof.

3 • Slide the shingle ripper up under the remaining shingles and pull the nails used to hold the old shingle. An alternative to pulling the nails is to hacksaw them off.

4 • Measure the width of the space left by the shingle or shake.

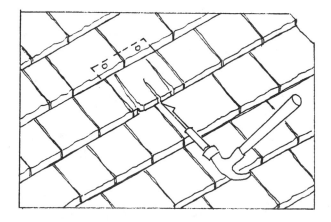

Removing a damaged wooden shingle.   (F)

5 • With your shingle hatchet (or a hammer and chisel) split off enough of the new shingle or shake so that it is between ⅜″ and ¼″ narrower than the space it must fill. (Illustration G) Wood swells when it is wet and the extra space is needed so the shingle or shake can expand.

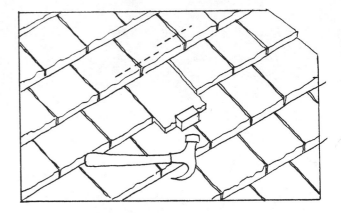

Replacing a wooden shingle or shake. (H)

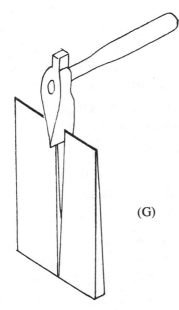

(G)

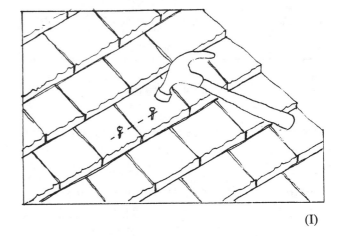

(I)

Cutting a replacement wooden shingle or shake.

6 • Push the shingle or shake into place. You can use a scrap of wood placed against its bottom edge and then tap the scrap with your hammer or hatchet. Be sure the bottom of the new piece is level with the shingles or shakes on either side of it. (Illustration H)

7 • The shingle or shake must be fastened with two 5d nails that are positioned from 1″ to 1½″ from its bottom edge and ⅜″ from the sides. If you are nailing shingles you will need 1¾″ nails. Shakes require nails 2″ long. The nails are driven through the

shingle on top of the replacement shingle or shake. (Illustration I)

Asbestos Cement Shingles

ASBESTOS CEMENT SHINGLES are heavier than asphalt shingles, so much heavier that the rafters must be reinforced to support them.

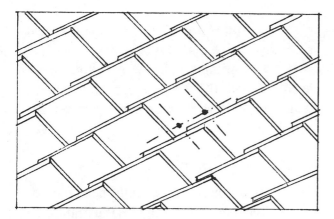

Marking the drilling position of a replacement asbestos cement shingle. (J)

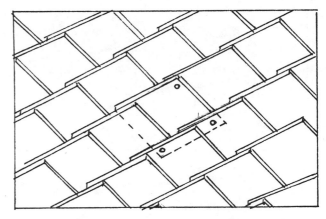

A replaced shingle in the Dutch lap pattern. (K)

They are fireproof and come in two designs and several colors. They have a tendency to crack, so when you walk on them, be careful to keep your weight on two or more shingles at a time. Like wooden shingles, asbestos cement shingles cannot be repaired. All you can do is replace them.

Replacing Asbestos Cement Shingles: Dutch Lap Pattern

1• Using a shingle ripper, remove the nails holding the damaged shingle, or hacksaw the nails in half.

2• Remove the damaged shingle.

3• Slide the replacement shingle into the vacant space.

4• Mark the drilling position with a hole punch and hammer for two nails. The marks should be 2″ below the butt line of the course above the replacement shingle, and 2″ in from each edge. (Illustration J)

5• Predrill the shingle for galvanized steel, stainless steel, or aluminum nails.

6• Nail the shingle in place. (Illustration K)

7• Cover each nailhead with roofing cement or clear butyl cement.

Replacing Asbestos Cement Shingles: Hexagonal Pattern

1• Using a shingle ripper, pull the nails holding the defective shingle, or hacksaw the nails in half.

2• Remove the defective shingle.

3• Slide the new shingle into place.

4• Mark the shingle in two places for nail holes using a hammer and center punch. The nail holes should be at least 8″ apart and 2″ in from the edge of the shingle. The nails do not go through any shingle other than the one you are installing.

5• Drill the replacement shingle and nail it in place, using galvanized steel, stainless steel, or aluminum nails.

6• Cover the nailheads with roofing cement or clear butyl cement.

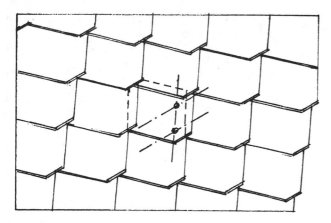

Position of nails in hexagonal pattern of asbestos cement shingles.

Slate Shingles

SLATE IS FIREPROOF. Slate shingles are also very heavy and require a specially supported system of rafters and other framing members to carry their extreme weight.

Slate roofs rarely need to be replaced, but if there are major repairs to a slate roof, consider hiring a roofing contractor to do the job for you. The material is heavy and awkward to handle and can easily break during normal handling.

Tools and materials • Working with slate requires a shingle ripper, putty knife, hacksaw, shingling hatchet or hammer and chisel, center punch, electric drill, roofing cement and galvanized nails.

Repairing Slate Roofing

You can fill cracks in the surface of slate roofing tile with roofing cement or clear butyl cement. Apply the cement liberally and smooth it with a putty knife.

If a slate shingle is loose or slightly damaged, lift off the loose piece and coat its underside with roofing cement, then replace the piece.

Replacing a Slate Shingle

1 • Using a shingle ripper, pull the nail holding the damaged shingle. (Illustration L) The nails can also be cut by sliding a hacksaw blade under the damaged shingle.

2 • Remove the slate shingle and measure the space to be filled.

3 • Cut the replacement shingle to size:

a) Scratch both surfaces of the slate with a chisel, using a straightedge as a guide. Be sure the scratches are opposite each other.

b) Place the slate so that the scratch line is aligned with the edge of a workbench, or any flat supporting surface. (Illustration M)

c) Tap along the scored line with your chisel handle to deepen it somewhat. Then rap the unsupported side of the slate with your hand, a chisel, or hammer handle.

d) Trim any uneven edges along the break line by tapping them with a hammer. (Illustration N)

4 • Push the new slate into place. Align it with the slate on either side of it.

5 • Mark two positions for nail holes on the replacement slate, using a hammer and

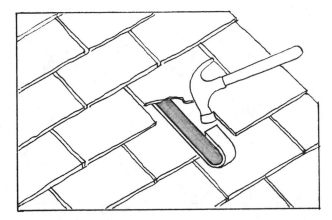

Replacing a slate shingle.　　　　　　(L)

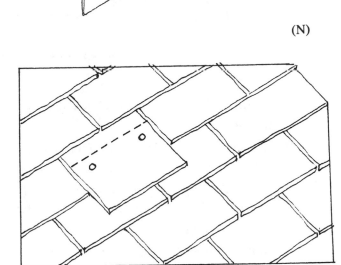

(N)

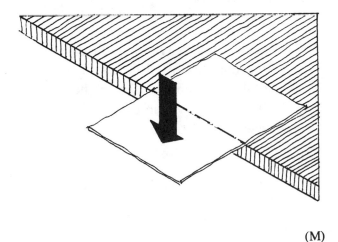

(M)

(O)

center punch. The marks should be 1″ below the butt line of the next higher course, and 2″ in from each side. (Illustration O)

6 • Drill the nail holes with an electric drill. You will be drilling though the new shingle and the shingle below it.

7 • Remove the replacement shingle.

8 • Coat the underside of the shingle with roofing cement.

9 • Slide the shingle in place again.

10 • Nail the shingle in place with galvanized steel or stainless steel nails.

11 • Coat the nailheads with roofing cement or clear butyl cement.

Replacing Slate Shingles with Straps

When the old slate has been removed and the replacement slate is ready to be positioned, it can also be held in place with copper or galvanized steel straps sold wherever you buy your slate.

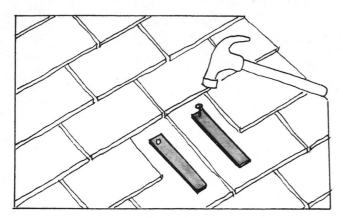
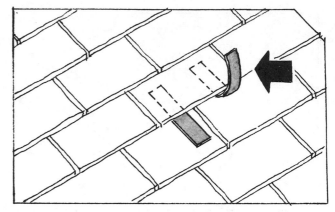

Metal straps can be used to hold slate shingles in place.

1•Place the metal straps on the slate under the replacement slate.

2•Using a single galvanized or copper nail at the top of each strap, nail the straps in place. Hit the nail with a quick, sharp blow. It will drive the nail through the slate without splitting it.

3•Coat the nailheads with roofing cement.

4•Slide the replacement slate into position.

5•The straps should be long enough to fold up over the. butt line of the new slate and extend about 2″ up the face of the slate. Fold them over the top of the slate and press them snugly against the stone.

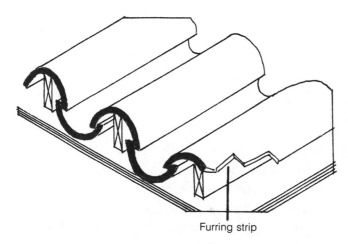

Furring strip

Mission tiles.

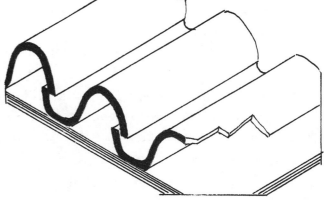

Spanish tiles.

Tile Roofing

THERE ARE TWO TYPES of tiles commonly used on roofs, Mission tiles and Spanish tiles, and while the difference in their design is minor, you have to know which you are dealing with so that you know where to nail them. *Mission tiles* are nailed to wooden 1″ × 2″ furring strips, which are stood on edge on the roof sheathing. *Spanish tiles* are nailed directly to the roof sheathing.

Spanish or Mission tiles cannot be repaired; they must be replaced.

Replacing Tiles

1 • Hook your shingle ripper under the tile and pull the nail holding it. (Illustration P)

2 • Drive the shingle ripper by hitting its curved end with a hammer until the nail comes free.

3 • Remove the tile.

4 • Place the new tile in position.

5 • Do not use old nail holes. With an electric drill, predrill through the new tile and the tile above it.

6 • Nail the tile in place with a galvanized steel nail. Spanish tiles are nailed to the sheathing. Mission tiles are nailed at the top of their highest curve, into furring strips. (Illustration Q)

7 • Cover the nailheads with roofing cement or clear butyl cement.

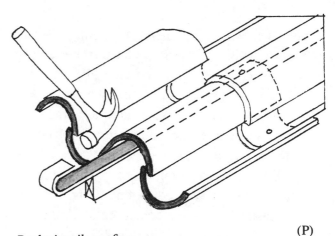

Replacing tile roofing. (P)

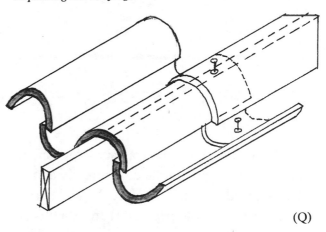

(Q)

Roll Roofing

ROLL ROOFING IS PAPER that is used to cover flat roofs. It has been saturated with asphalt and covered with mineral granules, and is available in several colors and weights. Usually a 75- or 90-pound weight is used for roll roofing, while 15- or 30-pound uncoated roofing paper is used as underlayment for shingled roofs. Most of the leaks that occur with a roll roofing occur along the horizontal seams or wherever there is flashing. When working with roll roofing, you must be careful that every nailhead goes squarely into the surface, so that it will not cut the paper. Be aware too that the material may crack as you're working if the temperature is too cool.

Tools and materials • The tools needed to work with roll roofing are a roofing knife, putty knife, galvanized roofing nails, asphalt or plastic roofing cement, and mineral-surfaced 90-pound roll roofing for patches.

Patching a hole of less than 2" in roll roofing.

MINOR REPAIRS TO ROLL ROOFING

When a leak develops in a flat roof, chances are that the point of entrance is directly above the damaged area in the ceiling. When you go up on the roof, you may find there is a blister or crack in the roofing cement along one of the seams, or a hole in the paper. Any of these conditions should be properly repaired.

Repairing Holes or Cracks Less than 1"

1 • Clean the area around the hole with a brush.

2 • Saturate a rag with kerosene and wipe the area. Allow the kerosene to dry.

3 • Fill the hole with roofing cement, using a putty knife. Coat the general area around the hole with a thin application of roofing cement.

Repairing Holes or Cracks Over 1" and Less Than 2"

1 • Brush the dirt from around the hole.

2 • Clean the area around the hole with kerosene.

3 • Fill the hole with asphalt roofing cement, using a putty knife.

4 • Cut a patch of 90-pound roofing paper that is 2" larger than the hole on all sides.

5 • Coat the underside of the patch with roofing cement. The underside is smoother than the upperside, which has uneven mineral chips in its coating.

6 • Press the patch down over the hole and nail the patch in place.

7 • Coat the edges of the patch with roofing cement.

Repairing Large Holes

1 • Remove the large hole in the roofing paper by cutting out a square or rectangle

from the roofing paper surrounding the hole. (Illustration R)

2 • Using the piece you have cut out of the roof as a pattern, cut an identical piece from 90-pound roll roofing paper.

3 • Brush the area to be patched and 6″ beyond each side.

4 • Clean the area you have brushed with kerosene and rags. Allow the solvent to dry.

5 • Coat the exposed sheathing with roofing cement. (Illustration S)

6 • Press the patch into the roofing cement.

7 • Fasten the patch to the roof with galvanized nails spaced every 2″ along its edges.

8 • Cut a second patch from 90-pound roofing paper, making it at least 4″ larger on all sides than the first patch.

9 • Coat the first patch with roofing cement. Be sure to cover all of the nailheads and the edges of the patch.

10 • Place the second patch over the first and nail it in place, spacing your nails 2″ apart and keeping them 1″ inside the edges of the patch. (Illustration T)

11 • Coat the edges of the second patch and the nailheads with roofing cement. Extend the cement at least 2″ beyond both sides of each edge.

Repairing Blisters

1 • Brush the area around the blister.

2 • Clean the area with kerosene or another solvent and rags.

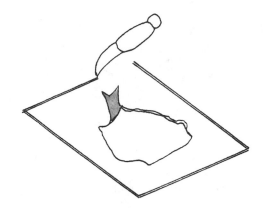

Patching a large hole in roll roofing.   (R)

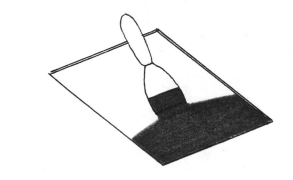

(S)

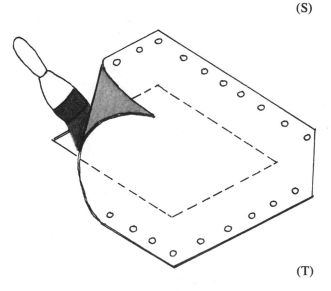

(T)

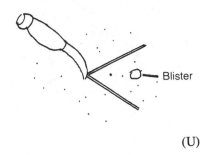

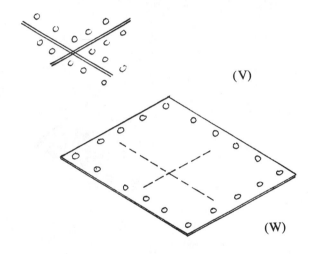

Repairing a blister in roll roofing.

6• Cover the nailheads and slits with a liberal coating of roofing cement.

7• Cut a patch from 90-pound roofing paper. The patch should extend at least 2″ beyond the cuts on all sides.

8• Press the patch over the cuts and nailheads.

9• Nail the patch in place, spacing your galvanized nails 2″ apart and keeping them 1″ from the edges of the patch. (Illustration W)

10• Cover the patch edges and nailheads with a liberal coating of roofing cement.

3• With a utility or a roofing knife, cut a slit through the center of the blister. One slice may be enough to flatten the paper. If it is not, make a right angle slice through the center of your first cut, forming a X. (Illustration U)

4• Dip your putty knife into the roofing cement and push the tar under all of the slices in the paper.

5• Nail down both sides of your cuts, using large-headed galvanized nails spaced no more than 1″ apart. (Illustration V)

MAJOR REPAIRS TO ROLL ROOFING

When the bulk of a flat roof is in disrepair, but not so bad that it must be replaced, it can be given a few more years of life by painting it with asphalt roof paint. The paint is less expensive than roofing cement and is sold in 5-gallons buckets, which will cover about 500 square feet. Apply roof paint in this manner:

1• Brush the entire roof clean of all pebbles and dirt.

2• All flat roofs have a slight pitch so that water will run off into the gutters. Begin applying the paint at the highest end of the roof and work down toward the lowest eaves. Apply the paint with a long-handled brush made specifically for roof paint.

3 • Brush the paint over a 5′ × 5′ square section at a time, working across the roof, and then back again. If the roof is reached by a hatch somewhere in its middle, leave a path to the hatch and paint your way off the roof, doing the area around the hatch last. The paint will dry in about two days.

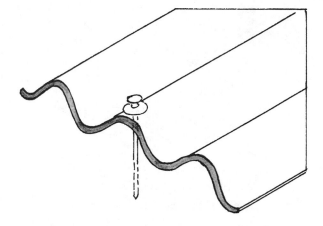

Place a washer under the head of each nail in a metal roof, to prevent water seepage.

Metal Roofs

METAL ROOFS ARE RARELY put on residences anymore. If you have a metal roof somewhere on your property, it should be painted every few years, and minor repairs made with roofing nails, asphalt cement, or solder and a metal patch. To install an entire metal roof requires at least a two-person crew and special equipment, so it is probably best to hire a contactor.

Painting a Metal Roof

1 • Using a wire brush and paint scraper, clean the entire roof of all loose paint and rust.

2 • Dust the metal clean.

3 • Paint all rusted or bared areas with a good-quality metal primer paint.

4 • When the primer has dried, paint the roof whatever color you wish, using a high-quality metal paint.

Renailing

If the roof must be nailed more securely, use galvanized steel nails with lead washers if the roof is made of galvanized steel. If the roof is aluminum use aluminum nails with any nonmetallic washer. With washers placed under the heads of the nails, it is not necessary to protect the nail with solder or roofing cement.

Repairing Pinholes

1 • Scrub the area around the holes with steel wool.

2 • Coat the area with acid flux.

3 • Heat the area with a propane torch.

4 • Spread melted solder over the pinholes.

Applying Small Patches to Metal Roofing

1 • Clean the area to be patched with steel wool.

2 • From the same material used on the roof, cut a patch large enough to cover the damaged area. Both galvanized steel and

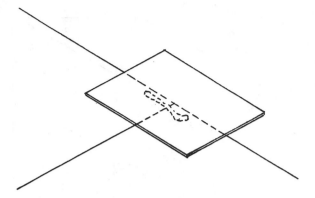

Applying a patch to metal roofing.

aluminum can be purchased in rolls and cut with tin snips.

3 • Apply an acid flux to the underside of the patch and the area to be covered.

4 • Heat the area to be covered and the patch with a propane torch.

5 • Apply a light coating of solder to both the area to be covered and the underside of the patch.

6 • Press the patch over the damaged area. Heat it with the propane torch.

7 • Check the edges of the patch carefully to be sure it is fully soldered. Apply more solder wherever there appears to be a gap.

Patching Metal Roofing with Roofing Cement

1 • Clean the area to be patched with steel wool.

2 • Using tin snips, cut a patch from whatever metal has been used on the roof.

3 • Apply roofing cement to the underside of the patch and the area to be patched.

4 • Press the patch in place.

5 • Apply roofing cement along the edges of the patch.

6 • If the patch does not appear to stay firmly in place, you may be able to nail it, using galvanized nails with lead washers (if the roof is galvanized steel) or aluminum nails with nonmetallic washers (if the roof is aluminum).

chapter 3

REPAIRS TO FLASHING, GUTTERS, AND DOWNSPOUTS

Flashing

IN MOST CASES when a roof leaks, the water makes its entrance through or under the flashing that protects the base of every chimney, dormer, skylight, vent pipe, and valley.

Flashing is currently made from a variety of materials, including roll roofing, lead, roofing paper, galvanized steel, aluminum, rubber, fiberglass, and neoprene, although you may be fortunate enough to have copper if your home is old enough to have been roofed before copper became expensive. The purpose of flashing is to prevent water from entering the house at any of the seams in the roof where different materials come together. The materials may be masonry, metal, and wood, all of which expand and contract in heat, cold, wet, and dry conditions at different rates. Since there must be a modest amount of space ($1/16''$) left between dissimilar materials to allow for their different rates of expansion and contraction, the flashing is used to span the joints and help to shed water from them as quickly as possible. You will find flashing under a properly installed roof at each valley, around the bases of dormers, skylights, vent pipes, and chimney, along the peak and wherever the roof meets a vertical wall. When it has been installed correctly, it can last for

35

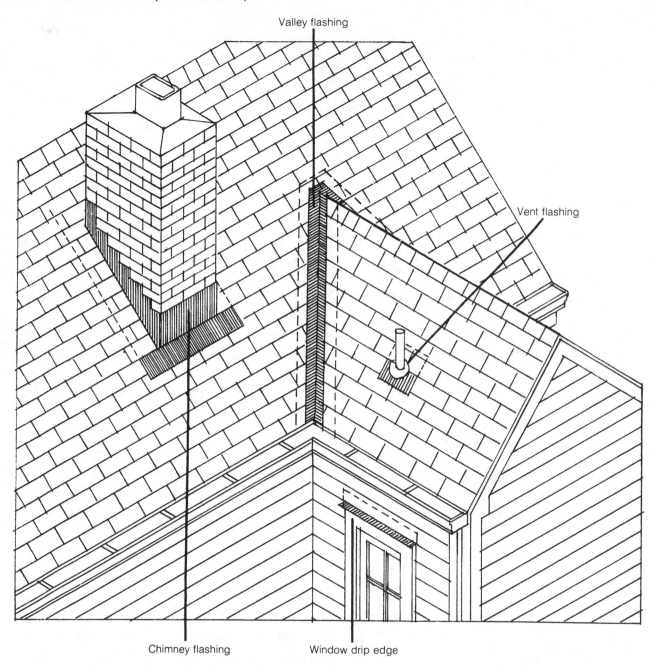

Valley flashing

Vent flashing

Chimney flashing

Window drip edge

The places where flashing can be found on your roof.

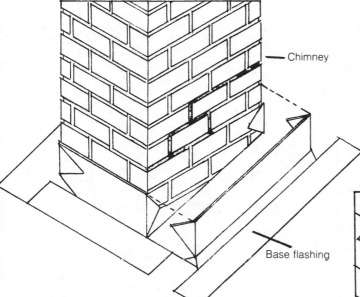

The structure of typical base (left) and cap (below) chimney flashing.

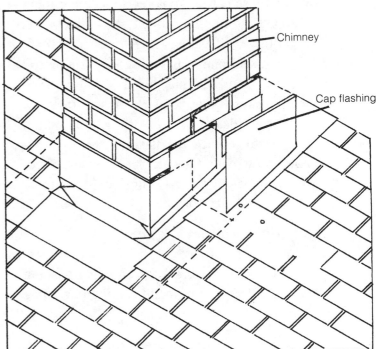

years without developing any leakage problems. But it can also incur hard-to-find pinhole leaks or cracks that admit gallons of water, or it can pull away from whatever surface it is covering to leave gaps or cracks that can be spotted and repaired without any great difficulty.

Flashing should be inspected carefully at least once a year for any signs of cracks or holes, or places where it has pulled away from a vertical surface. If you have doubts about the condition of any flashing, cover it with a coating of asphalt roof paint or asphalt cement.

Tools and materials • Among the tools you will need for repairing flashing include a hammer and chisel, a prize, putty knife, hacksaw, tin snips, pliers, and shingle ripper. The material you will use most often to make these repairs is roofing cement, although some caulking, principally some form of butyl, can also be relied on to do a creditable job.

CHIMNEY FLASHING

The flashing around chimneys represents perhaps the most common area of repair. It is constructed around the base of a chimney in two sections known as the base and the cap. The *base* extends partway up the side of the chimney and is also nailed to the sheathing under the shingles. The *cap* flashing covers the top edge of the base and is usually inserted into the mortar joints between the bricks that make up the sides of the chimney. After years of weathering, the cap may pull away from the chimney and literally provide a funnel for water running down the side of the chimney to continue right into the house. Holes also tend to develop at the corners of chimney flashing or wherever the metal has been bent, and while these can be repaired by coating them with asphalt roofing cement, the best repair is to replace the flashing altogether.

Some chimneys have asphalt felt or roll roofing paper flashing, but this will begin to melt eventually; as soon as you see streaks of tar on the sides of the chimney in your attic, it is time to replace the flashing, even if you have yet to detect a water leak. As a replacement, metal flashing is considered far more durable and waterproof.

Repairing Minor Holes in Chimney Flashing

Minor holes or cracks in chimney flashing can be filled with a liberal coating of roofing cement or a caulking sealant.

Refastening Chimney Flashing

1 • Carefully pry the cap flashing pieces away from the chimney. Do not damage the metal; if the flashing does not pull away easily, leave it imbedded in the mortar joint.

2 • Using a hammer and cold chisel, chip or scrape out all loose pieces of mortar in the joints. (Illustration A)

3 • You can fill the cleaned mortar joints with any caulking sealant that will adhere to brick and metal. (Illustration B) The ad-

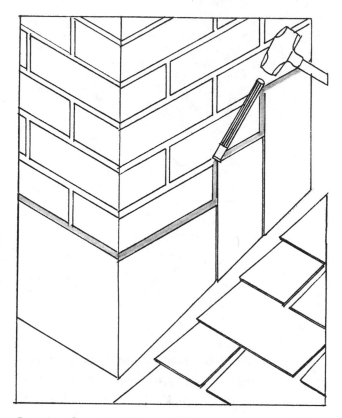

Steps in refastening chimney flashing.   (A)

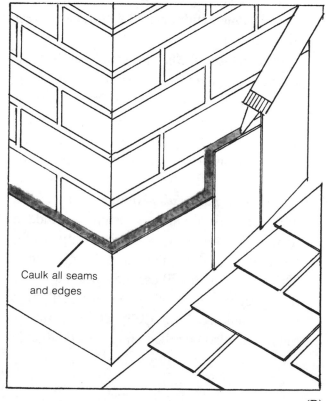

Caulk all seams and edges

(B)

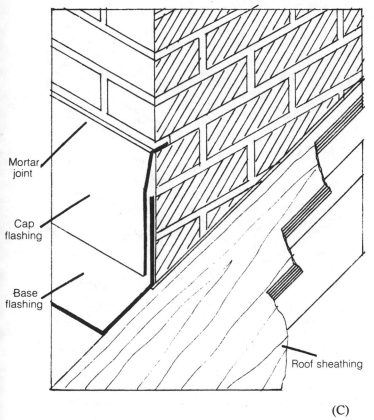

Mortar joint

Cap flashing

Base flashing

Roof sheathing

(C)

vantage to using the sealants is that you apply them with a caulking gun (see pages 95–96), which makes their application easier than applying roofing cement; roofing cement must be pushed into the joints with a putty knife.

4 • When the joints are filled, push the cap flashing back into the joints. If the flashing does not remain in place of its own accord, brace it with a brick or other heavy object until the caulking or sealant has hardened enough to hold it in place. (Illustration C)

See also "Installing Chimney and Ventilator Flashing" in Chapter 4.

Replacing Chimney Flashing

1 • Using a cold chisel and sledge hammer, chip out the mortar holding the cap flashing to the chimney.

2 • Beginning at the high side of the chimney, mark each piece of flashing with a number and remove each piece from the mortar joint that holds it.

3 • Carefully remove the shingles around the chimney. Use a crowbar or shingle ripper to remove the nails. Be careful not to rip any of the shingles, so they can be reused. Take off only enough shingles to expose the base flashing nailed to the sheathing.

4 • Beginning at the high side, number and remove each of the four sides of the base flashing. You will have to unfold the corners of each piece from around the chimney and remove the nails that hold it to the sheathing. Try not to damage the roofing paper under the flashing. (Illustration D)

5 • The best metal you could use to make new flashing is sheet copper, but it is costly. The second alternative is galvanized steel and the third is aluminum. Measure the various pieces you have removed from the chimney and calculate how much sheet metal you will need. You can purchase sheet metal in rolls of various thickness and length at hardware stores, plumbing supply outlets, and building centers, as well as at many lumber yards. Lay out each of the pieces you have taken from the chimney and trace it exactly on the sheet metal. Number your tracings according to the numbers on each piece. Cut out the pieces with tin snips and fold them according to the bends in their pattern pieces.

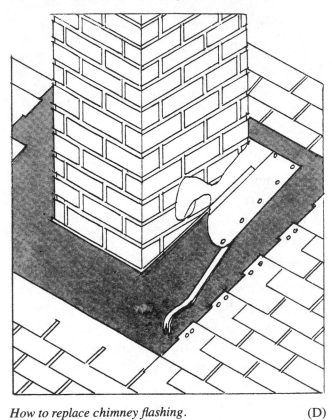

How to replace chimney flashing.

(D)

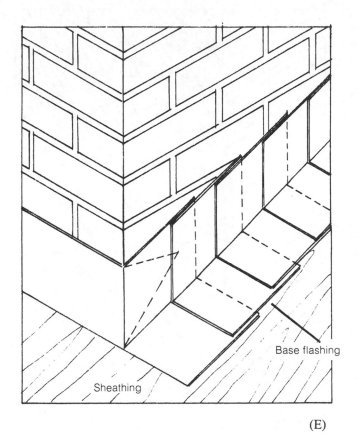

Base flashing

Sheathing

(E)

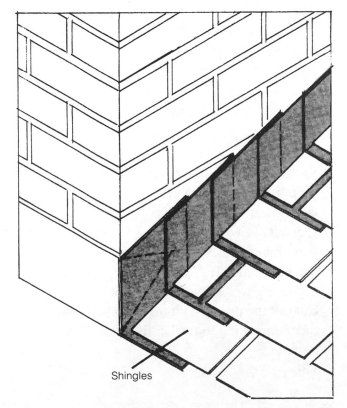

Shingles

(F)

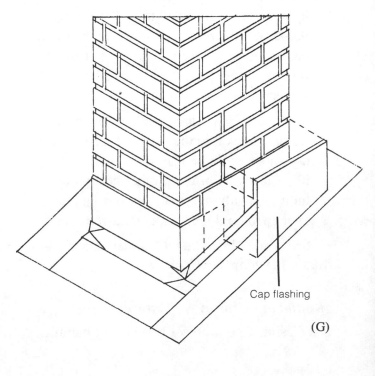

Cap flashing

(G)

6 • Begin assembly of the base flashing by installing the lowest side piece first. The bottom flange of the lower side is placed on top of the shingles and nailed to the sheathing. The nails must be the same material as the flashing or corrosion will occur at the nail holes. Fold the corners of the lower flashing around the chimney and cover all of its edges with sealant, be it roofing cement, clear butyl, or aluminized caulking compound. (Illustration E)

7 • Install the two side pieces of the base flashing. Fold their corners around the chimney and overlap the bottom of their flanges over the flange ends of the lower side flashing. The side pieces are nailed to the roofing paper that covers the sheathing. Cover all exposed edges and nailheads with roofing cement or whatever sealant you are using.

8 • Install the high side flashing last. It is nailed to the sheathing and its corners wrap around the chimney over the side pieces. Cover all nailheads and edges with roofing cement or other sealant.

9 • Replace all of the shingles you removed. (Illustration F)

10 • The top edges of the cap flashing pieces should be bent at least 1½″ to fit into the mortar joints in the chimney. Be sure the joints are cleaned of all loose mortar and are deep enough to accept the cap pieces. Install the lower side piece first by coating the inside of the metal with roofing cement or sealant and pressing it against the chimney. Hook its flange into the mortar joint and fill the joint with sealant or roofing cement, whichever you are using. (Illustration G)

11 • Working up from the bottom side, attach each of the side cap flashing pieces. Each piece is coated on its underside with sealant, each is inserted in the mortar joint, and each overlaps the piece below it. Seal all of the mortar joints.

12 • Attach the high side piece last and seal its mortar joint with roofing cement or sealant.

13 • Seal all exposed edges with roofing cement or sealant.

VENT PIPE FLASHING

The flashing around vent pipes used to be lead. Now you can purchase metal boots that

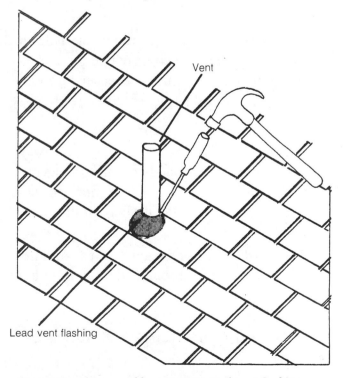

Vent

Lead vent flashing

Use a screwdriver and hammer to reseal vent flashing.

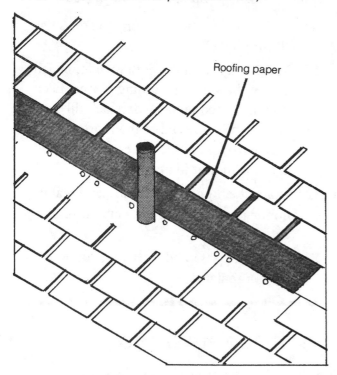

Installing a flashing boot over a lead vent pipe.　　(H)

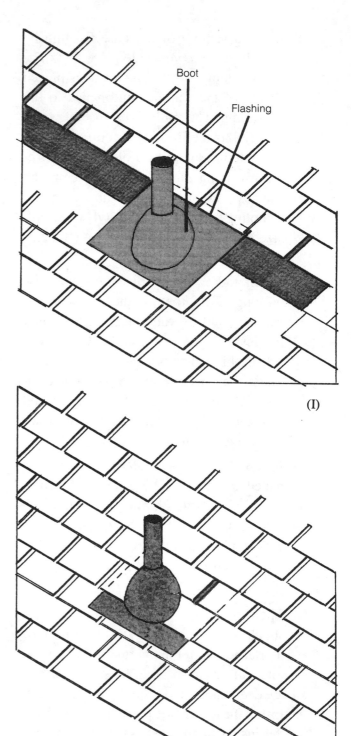

have a neoprene gasket around the hole in their neck, or are composed of two-piece plastic boots, both of which are easier to install than lead and will last longer too.

Resealing Vent Flashing

Lead vent flashing sometimes pulls away from the pipe it surrounds and allows water to trickle down the outside of the pipe and into your house. Reseal the flashing in this manner:

1 • Press the blade of a screwdriver against the top edge of the flashing and tap it with a hammer, forcing the lead back against the pipe.

2 • Cover the lead liberally with roofing cement.

Replacing Vent Flashing

The surest method of preventing leaks around a vent is to replace the flashing. This can often be done by purchasing a flashing boot large enough to cover the existing lead sleeve. The lead sleeve can be hammered down some to allow the boot to fit properly.

1•Remove enough shingles around the vent to expose about 6″ of the roofing paper that is over the sheathing. (Illustration H)

2•If the old flashing is to be removed, chip away the cement holding the boot and pull it off the pipe.

3•Clean the area thoroughly. If you tore any of the roofing paper around the base of the vent, patch it with 15-pound roofing paper (felt).

4•Slide the new boot over the pipe. Coat the base of the vent liberally with roofing cement and push the boot down until it is flush against the roof. Do not nail the flange as yet. (Illustration I)

5•Replace the shingles around the vent, nailing them in place. (Illustration J) Some of the nails should be driven though the flange on the boot. Coat each nailhead with roofing cement.

VALLEY FLASHING

The flashing placed in valleys, where two planes of a roof come together at an angle, is laid in three different ways and is then made open or closed according to how the shingles are laid over it.

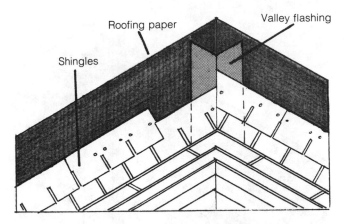

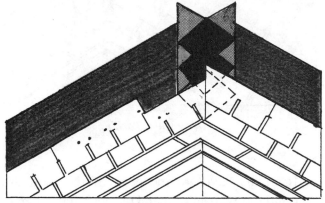

The two types of valley flashing used under closed valleys. Either a full piece of metal or metal squares can be used.

A *closed valley* is constructed by laying roofing paper up the full length of the valley and then covering it with a square, or overlapping squares, of copper, aluminum, or galvanized steel sheet metal. The shingles are then brought together to form a butt joint along the lowest point of the valley. If leakage develops along a closed valley, it is usually necessary to remove the covering shingles and replace the sheet metal. (See ''Installing Valley Flashing,'' Chapter 4.)

Open valleys are constructed by laying an extra layer of roofing paper along the valley

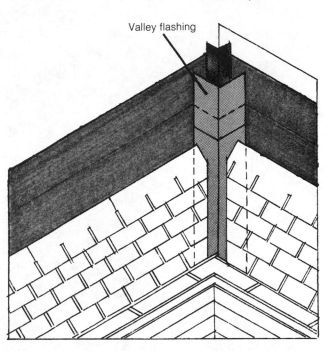

Open valley flashing.

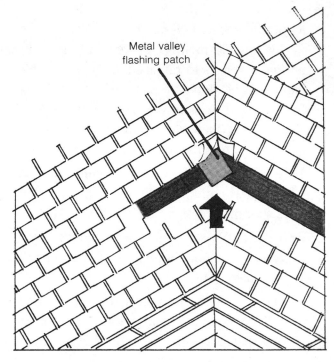

Patching a leak in closed valley flashing. (K)

from the eaves to the peak of the roof. A continuous sheet of metal (copper, galvanized steel, aluminum) is then placed over the paper. Alternatively, a series of sheet metal squares can be overlapped up the center of the valley. In either case, the shingles are not butted over the metal, but end an inch or so away from each other, leaving a metal trough running the full length of the valley.

The main purpose in having a closed valley as opposed to an open one is decorative, but, in fact, many experts consider the open valley more durable since water will tend to run down a metal trough quicker than it will uneven shingles. Open valleys are also easier to install since the critical butt joint need not have to be made with every course of shingles.

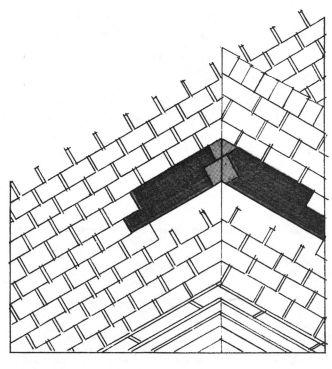

(L)

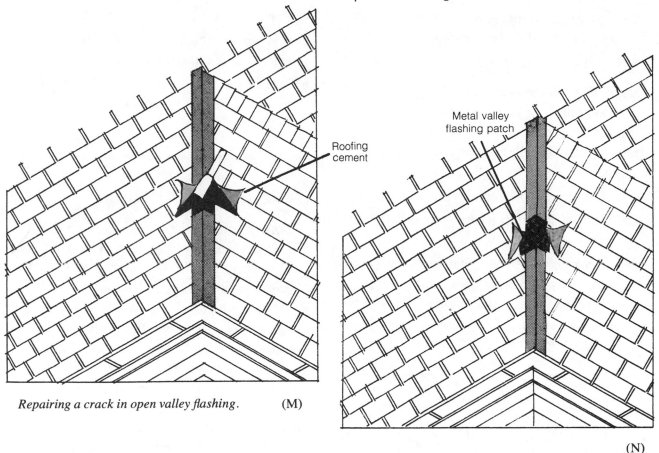

Repairing a crack in open valley flashing. (M)

Roofing cement

Metal valley flashing patch

(N)

Repairing Closed Valleys

Leaks in closed valleys can occasionally be repaired by removing the shingles in the area of the leak and patching the flashing with squares of copper, galvanized steel, or aluminum:

1 • Remove the shingles on both sides of the leaking area. Be careful not to tear the shingles; try to pull as many nails as you can.

2 • Cut a square of sheet metal from the same material used to make the valley flashing. The size of the patch will vary with the size of the damaged area, but it should be large enough to extend at least 2″ under the shingles above and below the ones you have removed. (Illustration K)

3 • Clean the damaged area in the flashing with a wire brush.

4 • Coat the damaged flashing with roofing cement.

5 • Bend the patch square to conform with the angle formed by the roof planes as they meet.

6 • Slide the patch square on top of the flashing and up under the shingles above the exposed area. If you encounter nails, they can be pulled or hacksawed in half. Position the patch over the damaged area. (Illustration L)

7• Replace the shingles over the patch, nailing them through the flashing.

8• Cover all nailheads with roofing cement.

Repairing Open Valleys

Small holes and cracks in open valley flashing are repaired in much the same manner as those in closed valleys except it is not necessary to remove any shingles:

1• Clean the damaged areas with a wire brush.

2• Coat the area with roofing cement. (Illustration M)

3• Cut a patch of sheet metal from the same material used to make the flashing (copper, galvanized steel, aluminum). The patch should be at least 1″ larger on all sides than the damaged area. (Illustration N)

Dormer flashing.

4• Bend the patch to fit the angle of the valley.

5• Slide the patch under the shingles on either side of the damaged area.

6• Weight the patch until the roofing cement has hardened sufficiently to hold the patch in place.

DORMER FLASHING

Dormers must have valleys along their bottom edges, where they rise out of the roof, as well as where their roofs meet the main roof. The flashing should extend up under the siding of the dormer and out over the shingles on the main roof. As a rule, the flashing is constructed of overlapping sheets placed first on the lowest part of the dormer, with each succeeding piece overlapping the one below it. Repairs to dormer flashing are made in the same manner as other flashing: small pinholes or cracks can be covered with liberal coatings of roofing cement. Larger damaged areas may entail removing some of the siding on the dormer or the shingles on its roof to get at the flashing and install a replacement piece.

Gutters and Downspouts

THE GUTTERS AND DOWNSPOUTS attached to the eaves of your home form a system for collecting water that runs off your roof and carrying it to the ground. The *gutters* are open troughs attached to the eaves of the roof and angled

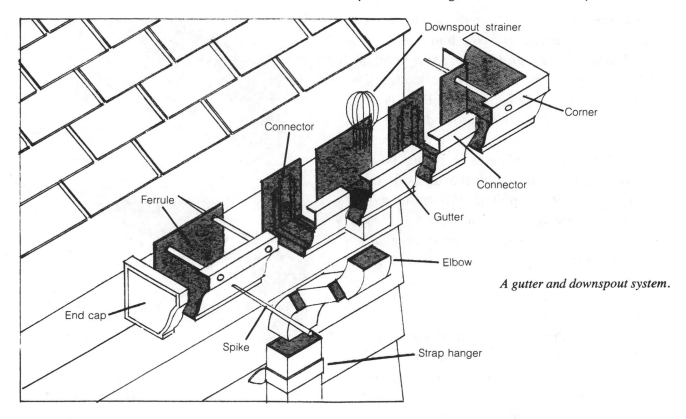

A gutter and downspout system.

slightly toward downspouts. The *downspouts* are pipes leading from low points in the gutter system to the ground. Downspouts empty onto the ground through an elbow that aims the water away from the house, or into a splash pan (usually made of concrete or stone) that helps to channel the water away from the foundation. Often, when a basement collects water after a heavy rain, it is because water coming from the downspouts is not being carried far enough away from the foundation.

Types of Gutters and Downspouts

Until recently, most homes used wooden gutters made by nailing two boards at an angle to each other. Wooden gutters demand constant inspection and frequent painting to keep them in condition, and when they must be replaced, they are usually discarded in favor of more durable, easier to maintain, aluminum or galvanized steel.

Metal gutters and downspouts • *Galvanized steel* gutters and downspouts are inexpensive, but subject to corrosion unless they are regularly protected with a rust-preventive primer. *Aluminum* gutters and downspouts cost more than galvanized steel, but they will not corrode. They are lighter than galvanized steel and more easily dented. Both types can be purchased with a durable white enamel finish baked on their surface, which eliminates the need to prime or paint the metal every few years. Both types are available in 10′ lengths, and building centers that sell them also carry a complete line of attachments and fastenings needed to assemble them on the eaves of your home.

Plastic gutters and downspouts • Within the past few years, polyvinylchloride (PVC) has been used to make gutters. PVC is extremely durable, will not corrode, and requires little or no maintenance. It will expand with temperature increases and must be attached with special hangers that allow for this expansion or it will pull away from the roof. PVC is also sold with a complete set of end caps, connectors, and other parts necessary for assembling a gutter and downspout system.

Gutter Fasteners

There are three ways in which a gutter can be supported under the eaves of a roof. Each is effective, and your use of any one of them is a matter of personal preference rather than any particular mechanical advantage.

Spike and ferrule • These are the professional choice since they are the easiest to install. The long aluminum spike is driven through the front lip of the gutter and inserted through a ferrule that spans the open top of the gutter, then it emerges through the back wall of the gutter, and is hammered into the fascia of the eaves. The ferrule prevents the sides of the gutter from collapsing.

Bracket hangers • There are numerous types of bracket hangers, but they are all attached to the fascia first, to form a cradle for the gutter. A separate strap is inserted over a tab in the top of the bracket and spans the open portion of the gutter, hooking over, or into, its outer lip.

Strap hangers • These are not nailed to the fascia, but to the roof sheathing, under the

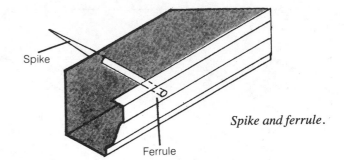

Spike and ferrule.

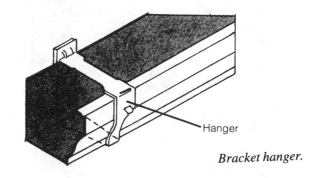

Bracket hanger.

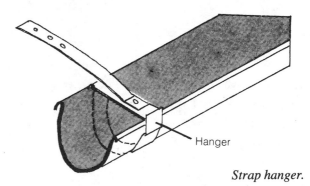

Strap hanger.

first course of shingles on the eaves. The strap portion spans the lips of the gutter, or, in another version, wraps all the way around the gutter. The strap hangers are best used when they can be applied to the roof before the shingles are put on, since it is hard to avoid cracking the shingles when bending them back far enough to nail the strap to the sheathing.

Maintaining Gutter and Downspouts

Given proper, regular maintenance, any

gutter system will provide years of service —but you must inspect them closely at least once each year.

Cleaning • In order to keep the system functioning properly, the gutters should be kept clean of leaves and dirt, as well as of the mineral granules that constantly wash off the surface of asphalt roofing materials. The best way to clean gutters is to roll up your sleeves and dig into the debris with your hands, and then flush out the residue with a garden hose.

Leaf strainers • Leaf strainers are shaped like a light bulb, but are made of metal wire or plastic strips. They are designed to fit into the mouth of downspouts, where they will catch large leaves, preventing them from clogging the downspouts. They are a useful addition to your gutter system, but if you install them they have to be checked periodically during the fall to be sure that leaves have not built up around them, blocking the flow of water into the downspouts.

Leaf guards • Leaf guards are sold in rolls and are nothing more than a narrow strip of mesh. The guard is pushed under the first course of shingles above the gutter and extends over the open portion of the gutter to hook under its front lip. Its purpose is to prevent leaves from falling into the gutter, and it works well if only a few leaves land on the roof and if the roof is not composed of new asphalt shingles. If there are a lot of leaves they will accumulate on the guard and cover it, preventing water from running into the gutter. If the roof is new the mineral granules carried off the shingles by running water will filter through the guard and build up in the bottom of the gutter without being washed away. As a result, you have to clean the roof

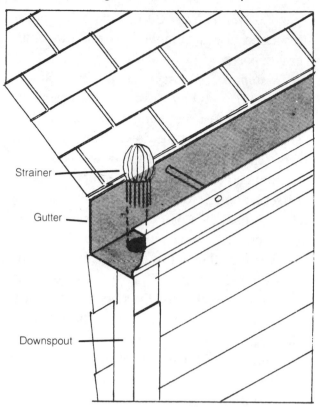

Leaf strainer (top). Leaf guard (below).

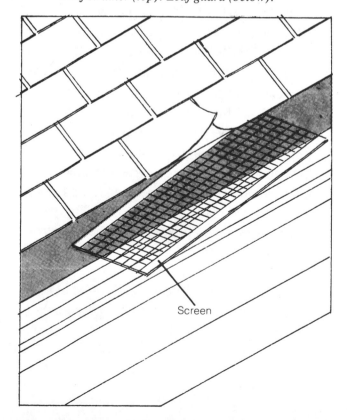

guard several times during the fall, and at least once a year remove it to get at the mineral deposits.

Unstopping downspouts • A downspout is fitted into a stubby downspout connection, which is part of the gutter run. It is attached simply by pushing the downspout up around the connector stub. But the downspout must be strapped to the side of the building, and to offset it enough to reside against the building there is usually a pair of 45° elbows inserted between the downspout and the connector. Leaves and other debris often get caught in the two elbows, clogging the downspout. The easiest way of clearing the stoppage is to push a plumber's snake down through the top of the downspout. Alternatively, you can dismantle the elbows and flush them clear with a garden hose.

Painting • It is best to leave copper gutters unpainted, even though the metal will take on the green color typical to copper as they age. PVC gutters need not be painted either. In fact, if the PVC has been properly installed to allow for its high expansion rate, you need only clean it once a year. Aluminum gutters have a baked-on enamel, so they rarely, if ever, need to be painted. You can extend the lifetime of galvanized steel gutters and downspouts by painting them every other year or so, but allow them to weather for at least a year after they are first installed. The paint should be given an undercoat of metal primer or it will flake off.

The best paint to use on the inside of wooden gutters is asphalt roof paint. Thin the paint to brushing consistency by mixing 1 part thinner to 4 parts paint. Paint wooden gutters after several days of sunny weather so the wood will be reasonably dry; it is better to apply two thin coats of paint, rather than one thick application. The paint will flow into small cracks and holes in the wood and help to seal the grain from further deterioration. Be aware that asphalt roof paint will stain the wood and bleed through any paint applied over it, so do not let it get on the outside of the gutter if you plan to paint the outside with a conventional paint. The outside of wooden gutters should be sanded smooth to remove any scaling or blisters and then painted with two coats of exterior house paint.

Combating ice dams and snow buildups • In many areas of the country where the winters are severe, the roof of a house can become overburdened with the weight of snow. Moreover, water freezes in the gutters and the snow builds up on top of it to push its way under the shingles along the eaves, where it meets and soaks through the sheathing and into the house. The weight of all that snow and ice can, of course, loosen the hangers that hold the gutter or bend the gutter out of shape, particularly if it is made of aluminum.

One way you can prevent ice from building up along the eaves of your house is to brush it off as soon as the snow stops falling. If your house is a one-story dwelling, you can do this with a long-handled broom or a hoe. But it is dangerous and not very easy to climb a ladder to get at the snow drifting on the roof of a two- or three-story house.

An alternative to preventing ice dams is to make sure your gutters are clean before the first snowfall and to install soffit vents under the eaves as well as extra insulation under the eaves in your attic.

A second alternative to fighting off ice dams is to install electrical heating tapes along the roof overhang and in the gutter and downspouts. The tapes are normally sold in pairs, one for the overhang and the other for the gutter. When the tapes have been installed, you can lead them through a window and plug them into any indoor outlet, or run an electrical line out of the house and attach an exterior outlet under the eaves. With an exterior outlet, you can control the tapes with a toggle switch inside the house. The drawback to heating tapes is that someone has to remember to turn the tapes on when it begins snowing, and turn them off again when the roof is bare of snow.

Snow guards are sold in several designs to be attached to the roof along the eaves, and when in place resemble small railings. Their purpose is to prevent avalanches of snow and ice from sliding off the roof. If avalanches are a problem and you decide to install snow guards, they should be spaced evenly along the eaves, usually about 4' apart.

REPAIRS TO METAL GUTTERS AND DOWNSPOUTS

If the repairs to a gutter or downspout are extensive, it may be less time consuming and easier to replace them (see pages 57–63) than to apply several patches. But if it is simply a matter of stopping a leak, there are a few ways to do this:

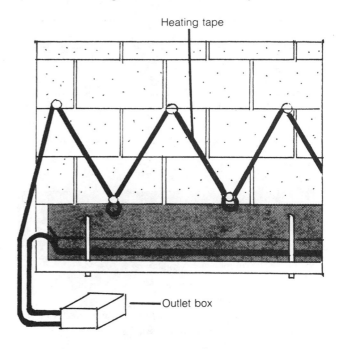

Heating tapes attached to a roof's gutter system.

Repairing Seams

Often, when a gutter leaks, the leak is coming from a seam, although the water may be dripping from the bottom of the gutter at a point several feet away. When you see water dripping from a gutter, trace it back to wherever it is emerging through the metal. If the leak is at a seam, apply a liberal coating of roofing cement or gutter caulking along the edges of the connector. If this fails to stop the leak, the connector can be replaced, or you can apply a patch over the area.

Repairing Pinholes

1 • Clean the damaged area with a wire brush or coarse sandpaper.

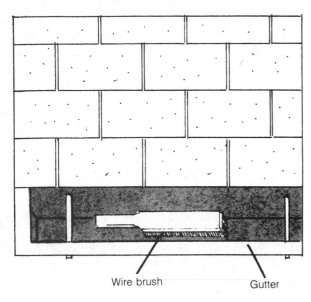

Wire brush   Gutter

Sealing a pinhole in a gutter involves cleaning the damaged area and applying roofing cement.

Repairing Small Holes or Cracks (¼" or Less)

1 • Clean around the crack or hole with coarse sandpaper or a wire brush.

2 • Wipe the area clean with a rag dipped in paint thinner.

3 • Cut a small patch large enough to cover the hole from thin sheet metal identical to the metal used in the gutter or canvas.

4 • Apply asphalt roofing cement to the damaged area.

5 • Place the metal or canvas patch over the hole. Press it into the roofing cement.

6 • Cover the patch with a liberal coating of roofing cement.

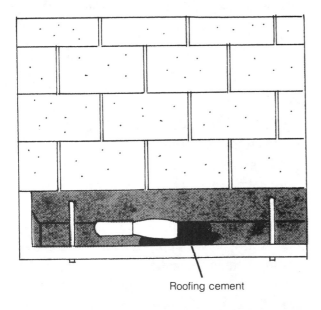

Roofing cement

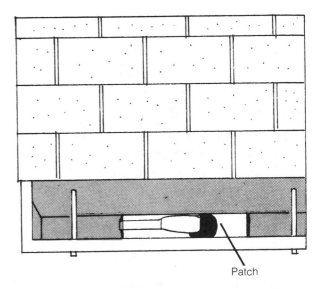

Patch

When patching a small hole, cover the patch as well as the damaged area with roofing cement.

2 • Wipe away all dust and grit with a rag soaked in paint thinner.

3 • Apply a liberal coating of asphalt roofing cement to the damaged area.

Repairing Large Holes (¼" or More)

1 • Clean the area around the damage with a wire brush or coarse sandpaper.

2 • Wipe the area clean with a rag dipped in paint thinner.

3 • Using the same metal used for the gutter, cut a large patch to cover the hole. (It is easier to first make a pattern out of paper). The patch should extend up the back of the gutter, across its bottom, and up the inside front, then wrap around the front lip.

4 • Bend the metal patch to fit the contours of the gutter.

5 • Coat the damaged area with roofing cement.

6 • Press the patch down over the roofing cement. It should extend beyond the damaged area by at least ½″ and fit snugly against all sides of the gutter.

7 • Using pliers, crimp the outer edge of the patch around the front lip of the gutter.

8 • Cover the patch with a thick application of roofing cement.

Fixing Downspouts

Downspouts are pipes attached to the underside of gutters and held in place by straps nailed to the side of the house. When a downspout splits, purchase a new length of pipe and replace it. If a leak develops at any of the joints between the downspout and the 45°-angle elbows that connect it to the gutter, it often can be sealed by applying gutter sealant or roofing cement.

The bottom of a downspout is usually connected to an elbow that is aimed away from the house. The elbow is under considerable pressure whenever water is pouring down the pipe and often works loose. It can be held to the downspout with a bolt:

1 • Drill a hole large enough to accept a lag bolt through one side of the elbow and the downspout.

2 • Drill a similar hole through the opposite side of the elbow and the downspout.

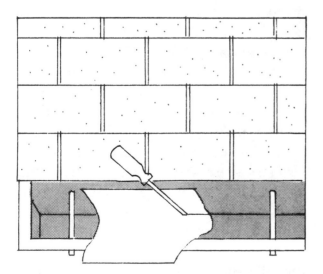
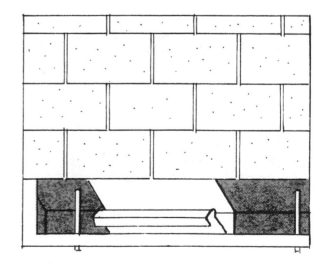

Applying a metal patch to a large gutter hole.

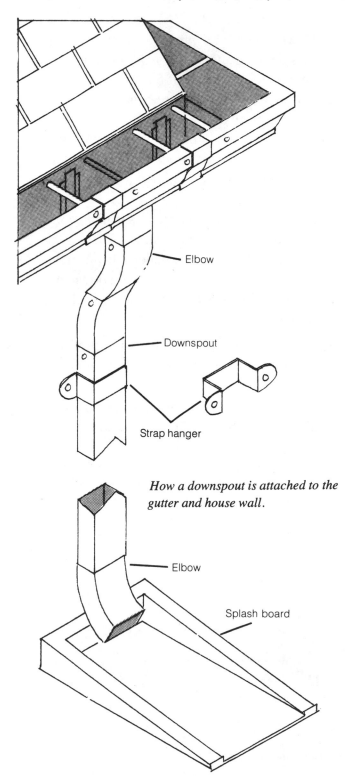

Elbow

Downspout

Strap hanger

How a downspout is attached to the gutter and house wall.

Elbow

Splash board

3 • Insert a lag bolt through the holes. Tighten the nut on the bolt.

CARRYING WATER AWAY FROM THE FOUNDATION

It is mandatory that all water draining from a roof be carried far enough away from the side of the house so that it will not permeate down to the foundation wall and seep into the basement. A basement that accumulates water during or after a heavy rain can often be kept dry by making certain that the downspouts empty sufficiently far away from the house—"sufficiently far" means at least 10'. There are a number of ways of handling the overflow from your roof so that it will not seep into the basement, but they all depend on one important element: the grading around the foundation walls must slope away from the house.

Foundation grading • When your house was first constructed, the land was graded so that it sloped away from the foundation walls. As the years passed, the house settled in its foundation and the natural process of erosion wore away the ground. It is possible that the land now slopes *toward* the foundation, with the result that any water running off the roof has a natural path toward the house, where it can then trickle down to the level of the basement floor. Moreover, if the downspouts have been allowed to simply empty into the ground beside the house, countless gallons of water most likely have worn down the soil directly under the downspout. While you can go around the house and readjust the downspouts, if the soil is not regraded you will not completely eliminate a wet basement.

Regrading the foundation of a house is thankless, back-breaking, time-consuming toil. If there are no plants along the foundation wall, the work is miserable enough all by itself. If you have shrubbery, flowers, vines, or anything else growing next to the building, the task can become a minor nightmare. The only good thing that can be said of regrading around your foundation is that the basement will probably remain dry and you will never have to do it again.

1 • Dig up all the foliage within 10′ of the foundation wall.

2 • Dig a trench 1′ deep and 10′ wide the full length of each wall.

3 • Grade the bottom of the trench so that it slopes 1″ for every foot of its width. Compact the earth with a tamper or heavy roller.

4 • Lay a sheet of 4-mil plastic on the graded trench. If you need more than one sheet to cover the width, the first layer is placed along the lower edge of the trench. The second sheet overlaps the first by at least 12″. The third overlaps the second by 12″. When you reach the foundation wall, coat the wall with a thin layer of roofing cement and stick the plastic sheeting to the cement. The sheeting should go up the wall to a point about 10″ or 12″ above the bottom of the trench.

5 • Fill in the trench. You can replant the shrubbery at this point, but when the trench is refilled it must also be graded 1″ for every foot of width and it is easier to compact the soil and grade properly if there are no plants to get in your way.

6 • Grade the topsoil of the trench 1″ for every foot of its width away from the house.

7 • Replant your shrubbery; most small plants and bushes can thrive in a foot of earth. Any water striking the soil will seep down as far as the plastic and then roll away from the house.

Splash blocks • When the grading around the foundation is correct, you still do not want the runoff to land in one place. Ready-made concrete splash blocks placed under each downspout will help direct water away from the foundation.

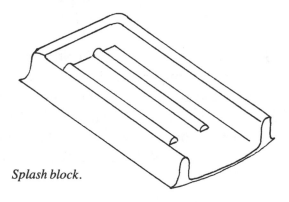

Splash block.

Perforated sleeves • Perforated sleeves made of either fiber or pipe can be added to the end of a downspout. The sleeve can be as long as you wish (preferably 10′, although that length may be impractical for your space). Some sleeves are made of plastic wrapped around a spring coil that forces the sleeve to roll up against the downspout unless it is filled with water. As water enters it, the sleeve unrolls and the water squirts out of perforations in its top.

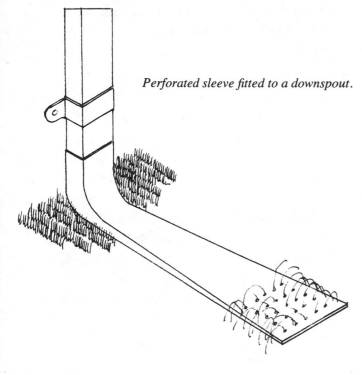

Perforated sleeve fitted to a downspout.

Drywells • An ideal way of getting rid of rainwater is to empty each downspout into a 4″ pipe that leads underground to a municipal sewer or to a disposal field that is at least 10′ away from the house. The pipe is not difficult to bury in the ground, but connecting it to the sewer may be next to impossible. So the alternative is to dig a drywell.

Drywells are no fun either. They must be at least 10′ away from the house and a minimum of 3′ square and 6′ or 7′ deep. Fortunately, two drywells are sufficient to handle the runoff from an average-sized house.

1 • Dig at least 10′ away from the house, and opposite a downspout. The ideal-sized hole should be 3′ × 6′–8′ and 6′–7′ deep. That's a lot of dirt to get rid of. Some of it could be used to steepen the grading around the foundation walls.

2 • Fill the hole to within 18″ of ground level with rocks, chunks of cinder blocks, bricks, gravel, anything bulky. Some experts prefer to cut off the top of a 55-gallon drum and punch holes in its sides and bottom, then fill it with rocks, but the drum is really not necessary.

3 • Dig a sloped trench from the top of the rocks in the hole to the downspout. The trench should slope 1″ for every foot of its run and be about 5″ wide. Compact the earth evenly in the bottom of the trench.

4 • Lay a 10′ length of 4″ PVC drainpipe in the trench. One end of the pipe should be in the center of the rocks in your hole. The other end has a PVC drain elbow solvent-welded to it. The elbow points upward and accepts the bottom of the downspout.

5 • Cover the drainpipe with soil.

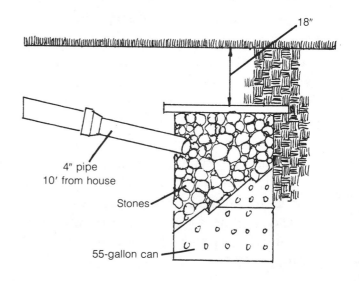

18″

4″ pipe
10′ from house

Stones

55-gallon can

A drywell can be a 55-gallon can or simply a hole in the ground with a cover over the rocks.

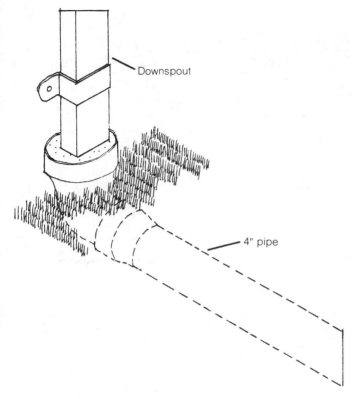

A drain elbow connects the downspout with a pipe leading to the drywell.

6 • Cover the rocks with a large flat stone or exterior grade plywood board to prevent soil from working down into the drywell.

7 • Fill in the top of the drywell with compacted soil and replace the sod, or plant grass, even shrubbery, over the well.

The runoff from your roof will fill the drywell from time to time, and the water will trickle out of the well in all directions, well away from the foundation. If the grading around the foundation is properly sloped, and especially if there is plastic sheeting under the topsoil, and if most of your downspouts empty into drywells, the chances of your basement flooding during even the heaviest rainstorm are practically nil.

REPLACING A GUTTER SYSTEM

When a gutter system deteriorates to the point where too many repairs are needed to make it watertight, it is simpler to replace all or most of the sytem. Unless you feel strongly about preserving the architectural design of your house, you will have less maintenance work in the future if you replace wooden gutters with galvanized steel or aluminum.

Calculating Materials

Metal gutters and downspouts are sold in 10′ lengths that can easily be cut with a hacksaw, and some brands can be found in lengths up to 30′. The most accurate way of determining how much to buy is to remove the old gutter system, count all the connectors, downspout outlets, corners, elbows and hangers, and end caps, then measure the length of each gutter and downspout section. If you are replacing wooden units with metal ones, the gutter and downspout lengths will remain the same, but you will have to compute the different components you need to assemble the sections.

No matter what your present gutter system may be, reckon on placing one downspout for each 35′ running feet of gutter; the downspouts will probably require an offset elbow to bring them from the roof overhang to the side of the house. You will also need a gutter hanger for every 3′ of gutter run and at least two straps to hold every downspout against the house siding.

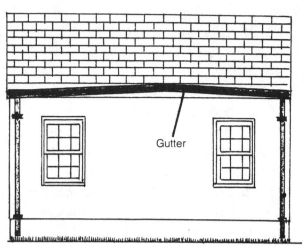

Every gutter must slope toward a downspout.

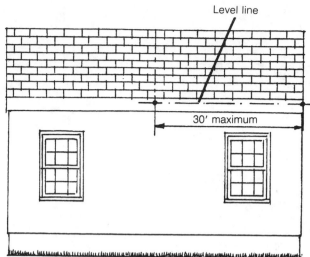

Measuring the length of a gutter run.

If you are replacing only part of a gutter system, take a portion of the old gutter with you when you go shopping to make sure you buy a compatible design. Gutter and leader designs change slightly from time to time, and if you are replacing a 20-year-old system, you may not find an exact match, but you can come close if you have a piece to compare.

Estimating the Slope of a Gutter Run

Gutters must slope toward their downspouts between $1/16''$ and ¼″ for every running foot. If a gutter run is more than 40′, there should be a downspout at each end, which means the center of the run will have to be higher than the two ends. In order to determine the slope of any gutter, the first rule to remember is: Do not assume the roof is level.

1 • Measure the length of the run and determine which end (or the center) will be the high point.

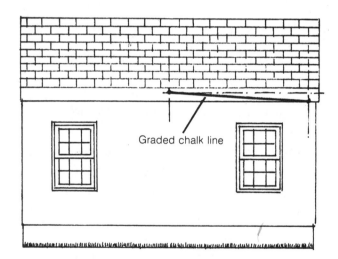

Chalk lines help determine the slope of a gutter run.

2 • Place a pencil mark on the fascia ½″ below the eaves edge at the highest point in the gutter run.

3 • Tack the end of a chalk line at the mark.

4 • Hang a line level from the chalk line and stretch the line to the low end of the run.

5 • Level the chalk line and tack it to the fascia.

6 • Measure the length of the chalk line.

7 • Reckon an average of ⅛″ for each foot of the string length. Add up all of the ⅛ths.

8 • At the low end of the gutter run, measure the total number of ⅛ths down from the chalk line and mark the fascia.

9 • Move the low end of the chalk line down to your new mark.

10 • Take off the line level and snap the chalk line.

11 • Repeat steps 1–10 for the gutter run between every downspout.

Assembling Metal Gutters

Lengths of gutter are assembled with connectors that have flanges that the gutter slides into, but which must also be caulked. Consequently, most of your assembly work should be done on the ground. You have to be careful when you are cutting pieces of gutter that you measure accurately and include the width of the connectors.

Cutting metal gutters • Enameled gutters should be cut with tin snips so that the enamel is not chipped. Unfinished gutters can be cut with either tin snips or a hacksaw, but if you are using a hacksaw, it will tend to distort the metal. You can prevent this distortion by placing a piece of 2″ × 4″ lumber inside the gutter at the point you are sawing. Wherever you have cut the metal, there are likely to be small burrs left along the cut edges, which should be filed off with a fine-toothed metal file so that the edges will slide easily into the slip connectors.

Drilling • If you are hanging the gutter system with spikes and ferrules, it is best if you

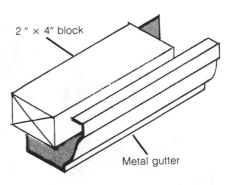

2″ × 4″ block

Metal gutter

Place a block of wood inside a gutter anytime you are cutting or drilling the metal, so that you do not dent it.

drill holes for the spikes in the front lip of the gutter before you get up on a ladder to nail the gutter in place. The spikes should be placed every 3′ and can be hammered through the back wall of the gutter as it is being installed, but if you have to punch a hole through the front lip at the same time, the metal may collapse and leave an unsightly dent. To prevent this:

1 • Before drilling through the gutter, slide a piece of 2 × 4 inside it for support.

2 • Mark where you want to drill by hammering a hole punch against the metal. This will protect the drill bit from ''walking'' when you first press it against the metal.

3 • Drill holes every 3′ in the front lips of all gutters. Drop outlets for downspouts should have a hanger placed at each end of the connection. Corners should have one spike placed at each side of the L.

Making connections • Most metal gutter systems are assembled with slip connections that are first caulked:

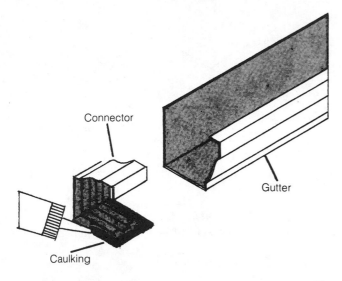

Connecting a gutter system. (O)

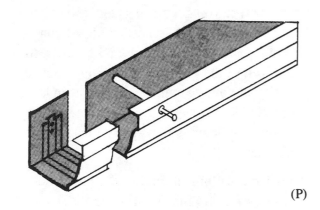

(P)

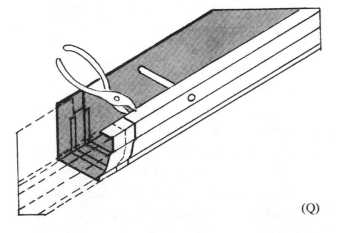

(Q)

1 • Measure and cut the gutters to be connected.

2 • Apply a liberal bead of caulking in the slot formed on the inside of the connector by its interior flange and the inner wall of the connector. End caps have a bent slot around their perimeter that fits over the end of the gutter. The slot should be filled with caulking. (Illustration O)

3 • Push the connector or end cap over the end of the gutter. Be sure the gutter is completely seated. (Illustration P)

4 • When all parts are assembled to the coupling, fold its top edges over the lips of the gutters using a pair of pliers. (Illustration Q)

5 • Smooth the caulking that has oozed out of the connector joints with a putty knife so that water can flow over it and not be slowed by any obstructions.

Installing Gutters

Once a section of the gutter has been completely assembled, you can install it on the fascia. The finished gutter is, in effect, a watertight trough. It should have an end cap on any open end and every connection should be well caulked. If you have a downspout connector at the end of the run, it too must have an end cap on it.

The exception to the rule of having end caps at both ends of a gutter run is when the gutter must turn a corner and then continue along an adjacent side of the house. You may find it is easier to install the corner in place against the house and connect the gutters to it as they are being put in place. You can attach slip connectors to either the end of the gutter or the ends of the corner, caulk them, and then bend their edges down after the gutter is in place against the house.

Installing gutters is at the least a two-person job, with one worker at each end of the gutter to lift it in place and attach it with whatever hangers are being used. The gutter itself is flimsy and will not achieve any rigidity until it has been completely secured against the fascia.

1 • If bracket hangers are being used, these should be installed along the chalk line before the gutter is brought up to the fascia. If spike and ferrule hangers are used, insert a spike through the predrilled hole in the front lip of the gutter and slide the spike into the ferrule. Position the ferrule at right angles between the lips of the gutter and hammer the spike into the fascia.

2 • If the gutter is to go around a corner, nail the corner to the fascia with one hanger on each end. The inner lip of the corner is placed exactly against the sloped chalk line.

3 • Using at least two workers, lift the gutter in position with its back lip against the chalk line. Slide its open end into the slip connector on the corner.

4 • Continue assembling your gutter runs and attaching them to the fascias around the house.

Assembling Downspouts

If your roof has a wide overhang, the downspouts will need two 45° elbows and a

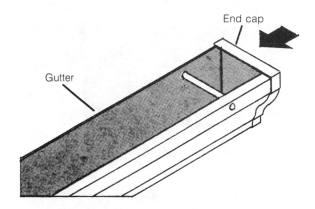

Caps are inserted over the end of the gutter.

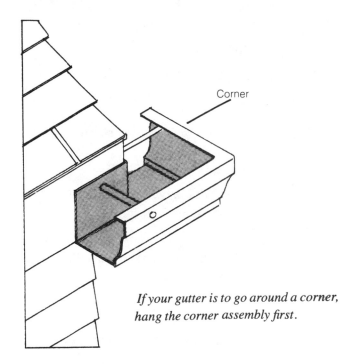

If your gutter is to go around a corner, hang the corner assembly first.

short length of downspout to bring it from the stub on the downspout connectors to the outside wall of the house. If the overhang is not a wide one, the downspout is connected simply by pushing it up around the connector stub. Follow this procedure to measure the overhang and install the downspout:

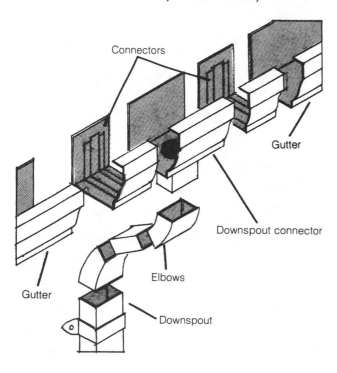

Downspouts are attached to connectors assembled in the gutter run.

1 • Measure the distance from the back of the downspout connector stub to the wall of the house. (Illustration R)

2 • Insert the elbows into each other and measure the distance from the outside of one curve to the inside of the other curve. In other words, measure the width of the assembly from the back of one pipe to the front of the other. (Illustration S)

3 • Subtract the measurement determined in step 2 from the width of the overhang determined in step 1. The result is the approximate length of pipe needed between the two elbows to bring the downspout from its connector to the wall.

4 • Measure and cut the short length of pipe.

5 • Assemble the elbows to the piece of pipe and insert one elbow over the downspout connector stub to make sure your measurements have been correct. (Illustration T)

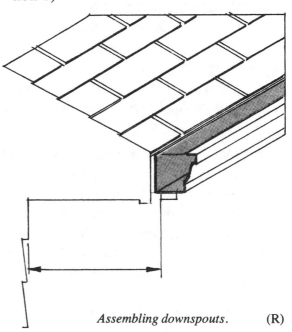

Assembling downspouts.   (R)

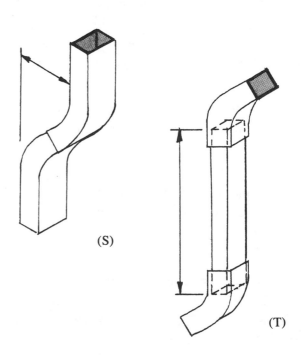

(S)

(T)

6· If the elbow connection fits so that the lower elbow touches the wall, remove it from the downspout stub and drill holes through opposite sides of each elbow for machine screws to hold the pieces together.

7· Install the attached elbows on the connector stub and measure the distance from the bottom elbow to the ground. Allow for enough pipe to fit over an elbow at both ends.

8· Cut a piece of downspout pipe to the required length, using a hacksaw.

9· Connect an elbow to one end of the pipe using machine screws.

10· Stand the downspout up under the elbows leading from the downspout connector and push it up over the lower elbow.

11· Downspouts are held to the side of a house by sheet metal straps bent around the downspout in the form of a U. The ends of the straps have holes in them for nails and are bent back to fit against the wall on either side of the downspout. Use galvanized roofing nails to attach the straps to wooden siding. The first strap should be about 1′ below the top of the downspout pipe. Space all other straps about 5′ apart.

If you are attaching downspouts to a masonry wall, you will have to drill holes in the masonry for lead plugs and then hold the straps in place with screws.

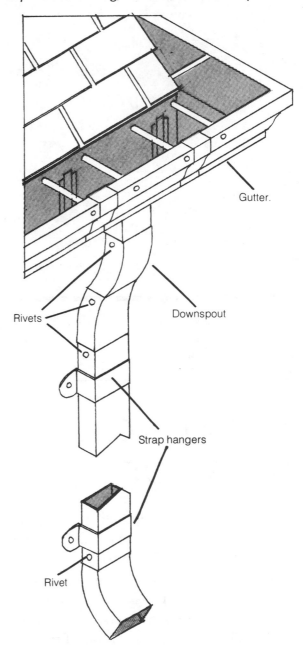

Downspouts are secured to the side of a house by U-shaped metal straps.

chapter 4

INSTALLING A NEW ROOF

THE ULTIMATE REPAIR to the outside of your house is to install a new roof. Most municipalities state in their building code that no roof shall have more than two layers of shingles because more than that could place too much weight on the rafters. As a result, you can reshingle your roof one time by merely laying new shingles over the existing ones. You can even change roofing materials, for example, put asphalt shingles over wooden shakes. But the next time you need to reshingle, at least one of those layers must be removed, and if you are going to take off one

layer you might as well remove them both. By taking off both layers, you will probably ruin the building paper that was laid over the sheathing, so that too should be replaced. Even if it is in fairly good condition, it has had a great many nail holes poked through it over the years and probably can no longer function as an effective barrier against moisture. Now you are down to the sheathing, which, if wooden shakes or shingles were originally installed, may consist of $1'' \times 6''$ boards spaced $2''$ apart across the rafters. If you intend to install modern asbestos or asphalt shingles, the sheathing must be closed, not open (see page 68) so you will either have to insert more boards in the spaces, or take off the existing sheathing and cover the rafters with exterior-grade plywood. In addition, take a close look at the fascia that is nailed to the rafter ends, and at the gutters and downspouts that are attached to it. The gutters may be about ready for replacement, and the fascia may have developed some rot from years of being wet. It is only a $1'' \times 4''$ pine board; you might as well replace it and provide yourself with a solid base from which you can hang a new gutter. (See "Replacing a Gutter System," Chapter 3.)

It takes two men with crowbars less than a day to rip the entire roof off an average house. Obviously, if people are living in the house, you may want to dismantle only part of the roof at a time and put the new sheathing down as you go so that the building is protected at all times. For the sake of continuity, the procedures given in this chapter do not take into account the fact that it might rain before you complete your reroofing, or that you might get bored with it all and decide to take the afternoon off and go fishing. It is a good idea to reread chapters 2 and 3 before attempting to do a whole reroofing, so you have a clear picture of the roof and gutter systems.

ESTIMATING MATERIAL AND COSTS

The cost of replacing an entire roof includes the cost of the following essential items:

Roofing material (shingles, shakes)
Roofing paper
Sheathing
Roofing cement
Nails
Equipment rental
Flashing materials (sheet metal)
Boards (for repairs to the roof edges)

The cost of the roofing materials, roofing paper, and sheathing amount to roughly 90%

of your costs, so you can arrive at a reasonable guestimate by figuring the amount of those materials and adding them together.

Roofing materials, that is shingles and shakes, are sold in squares, or portions of a square. A square is 100 square feet. Shingles are so heavy that they are normally sold in bundles that contain enough material for one-third or one-quarter of a square.

But, before you order any roofing material you have to know how many squares are in your roof. That means you have to go up on the roof and measure its square footage. You will find that your roof, like everyone else's, contains one or more rectangles, triangles and/or trapezoids. Determining the exact areas of all these can become cumbersome, so don't bother. You will arrive at almost the same dimensions by reducing each surface to simple rectangles and mulitplying their length times their width. In Illustration A, for example, treat the triangles labeled C, D, and E, and the trapezoid marked B as a single rectangle, which, in this case, equals rectangle A. Trapezoids D and E can then be handled as shortened rectangles of equal size. By simplifying the areas in this manner you may end up a little short of roofing material, but by the time you install what you have purchased, you will be able to tell exactly how much more you need and thereby avoid overbuying.

When you have measured the various rectangular surfaces that make up your roof and calculated their areas in square feet, add them together. The result will be the total number of square feet in your roof, which is divided by 100 square feet to give you the number of squares of material you need to

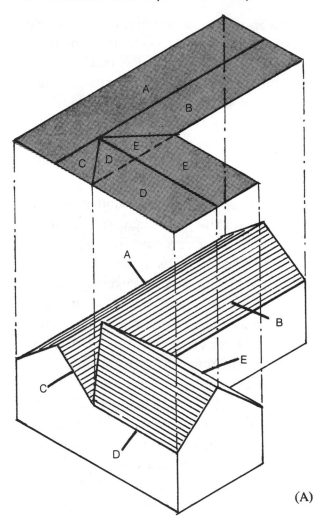

(A)

Reduce all of the planes in your roof to simple rectangles in order to determine the square footage of the roof.

buy. The shingles, shakes, and roofing paper you need are sold by the square or fraction of a square and each bundle, or roll, is labeled as such. The plywood or pressboard needed for sheathing comes in $4' \times 8'$ panels, which contain 32 square feet. Divide the total number of square feet in your roof by 32 to arrive at the number of panels needed for your sheathing.

SELECTING ROOFING MATERIALS

You can usually replace the roofing materials that are currently on your roof with similar materials. But if you decide to change from wooden shakes, for example, to asphalt shingles, there are several considerations that must be taken into account.

Pitch • Will the materials you want to install provide a weatherproof roof, given its existing pitch? The pitch of a roof is different from its slope. The *pitch* indicates the ratio of the rise of the roof (the vertical distance from the attic floor to the ridgepole) to the span of the roof (the horizontal distance between the side walls of the house). The ratio is expressed as a

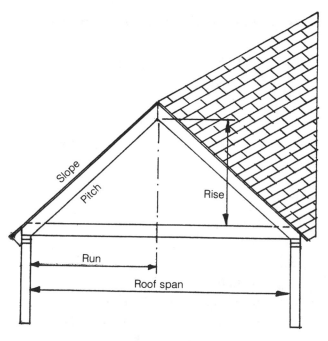

Locating the pitch and slope of a roof.

fraction, so if the rise is 8′ and the span is 32′, the ratio of the pitch is $^8/_{32}$, or ¼. The steeper the roof, the larger the fraction. Thus, ¼ is steeper than $^1/_5$ or $^1/_6$. The *slope* of a roof is also a ratio given as a fraction. But the slope pertains only to one plane of the roof defined as the ratio of the rise (vertical distance from the attic floor to the ridgepole) to the run (the distance from a side wall of the house to the center of the attic floor, directly under the ridgepole).

If the pitch of your roof is $^1/_5$ or steeper, you can use any roofing material to cover it— asbestos shingles, wooden shakes or shingles, asphalt shingles, slate, tiles, tar paper, anything.

If the roof pitch is $^1/_6$ or less, you are limited to covering it with roll roofing or hot mopped layers of tar paper with, or without, decorative rock and gravel. If the pitch is $^1/_6$, you can get away with asphalt shingles, but only because they lie flatter than other shingles or shakes. Low-pitched roofs invite heavy winds to work under shingles and shakes and tear them off the sheathing, so asbestos shingles, wooden shakes or shingles, and asphalt shingles are rarely installed on any roof with a pitch that is less than $^1/_5$.

Color, size, pattern • If you change the roofing material on your house, will the new material be architecturally compatible with the rest of the building? The color, pattern, and size of your roofing is a matter of personal preference. In making your choice, bear in mind that very large shingles may appear incongruous on a small house, as might a hexagonal pattern. There are also some colors on your roof that are not easily changed, such as the bricks or fieldstones in your chimney. The color of the roof itself ought to be compatible not only with the red or gray of the chimney, but with the sides of the house as well. So far as the shade of that compatible color is concerned, remember that if you live in a predominately warm climate, your house will stay cooler if you have a light-colored material on the roof that can reflect the rays of the sun.

Framing • Can the roof framing, as it stands now, support the added weight of your new roofing material? If the original roofing material was roll roofing, asphalt, or wooden shakes or shingles, the rafters were probably not constructed to hold the weight of slate, tiles, or asbestos shingles. If you are going to use any of the heavier materials, consult an architect or building engineer and get specific advice on how the rafters should be shored up to support the added weight.

Installation • Can you install the new roofing material yourself or must you hire a contractor? Anybody can install asphalt shingles, roll roofing, and wooden shakes or shingles. If you have the time and patience, as well as one or two assistants, you can probably also put up a slate, a tile, or a metal roof. But decorative rock and gravel on hot mopped layers of tar paper demands special equipment and considerable experience that is best left in the hands of an expert. And in most instances, you would be wise to hire an expert to install slate, tile, or metal as well. They are just too awkward to handle unless you have had some practice in working with them.

Cost • Will the new roofing and its installation fit into your budget? The easiest roofing materials to install—asphalt, wood, and roll roofing—are also the least expensive. An average-size roof might be reroofed for as little as $500 or $600 spent for materials. A contractor will charge another $1,000 or so to do the work, but a final cost of $2,500 or $3,000 for materials and installation would not be unusual. Asbestos shingles are even more expensive and difficult to install. Slate and tiles could run your roofing bill well into several thousand dollars, even if you did the work yourself. At least if you decide to put on asphalt shingles you can install the cheapest brand and be sure of a good, watertight roof that will last for years. Spend a little more for top of the line shingles and they will endure even longer. Cedar and redwood shingles and shakes, because of their natural resistance to decay, will always provide a lasting installation.

TOOLS AND MATERIALS

There are no exotic tools or materials needed to install shingles, shakes, or roll roofing. A *crowbar* or small *prize* is necessary to pry nails out of the old shingles. A *hammer* and *chisel* or a *shingling hatchet* are needed to dismantle wooden shingles or shakes. The hammer is also necessary to attach new materials. A hooked *roofing knife* can cut roofing paper as well as asphalt shingles, but so can *tin snips,* which you will need to shape flashing. You may also need a *chalk line* to mark straight lines across the roof and along valleys, a *folding rule* or *steel measuring tape* and at least one *ladder*. If your roof is steep, you can rent several sets of *triangular braces,* which are nailed to the roof and can be adjusted to any angle to support a plank that can be used as a *scaffold.*

Underlayment • On most roofs the underlayment is 15-pound roofing paper. It can consist of a dry felt, saturated felts, or heavy paper made of fibers impregnated with asphalt. The paper is sold in rolls 36″ wide and 108′ long (324 square feet). The weight of the paper is normally between 15 and 30 pounds per square. When you buy underlayment, purchase one with white lines drawn on its length. The lines on the paper, when it is laid out on the roof, become a guide for laying down shingles so that they form straight courses.

Sheathing • Depending on whether or not you are laying wood shingles or shakes or asphalt shingles, the sheathing will be either open or closed. Open sheathing consists of boards that are no more than 6 ″ wide spaced 1″ or 2″ apart across the rafters to permit air circulation under wood shingles or shakes so they will not rot. Solid sheathing can be constructed from boards butted together, or tongue and grooved, or exterior-grade plywood that can be ⅜″, ⅝″, ½″ or ¾″ thick. For most roofs ⅜″ plywood is sufficiently strong to support the roofing material.

Roofing cement • Roofing cement can be plastic or asphalt based, and you will need about a 5-gallon can to put shingles and flashing on an average-size roof. The correct cement to use with various mineral-surfaced roll roofing usually comes with the paper when you buy it. There are also numerous caulkings and sealants, such as clear butyl, manufactured for work on roofs. You may need some of these for touching up odd corners in your flashing, but when you are doing an entire roof, they can become quite expensive.

Nails and staples • If you are hanging wooden shakes or shingles or asbestos shingles, use 6d common nails that are 2″ or longer. Asphalt shingles and roll roofing require galvanized roofing nails. The nailheads are ⅜″ in diameter and nail lengths range from ¾″ to 2″. As an alternative with asphalt shingles, you can also use 1″-wide staples with lengths of ½″ – 1¼″.

Removing the Old Roof

As you proceed to remove the old roofing material, try not to damage the flashing around vents, dormers, and skylights, in the valleys, around chimneys, or wherever the roof meets a vertical wall. All of the old flashing, particularly if it is to be replaced, represents patterns for cutting new flashing, and if it is taken off the roof carefully it will save you considerable working time when cutting the new metal.

Also be careful not to destroy the sheathing, unless you plan to replace it. If, when the roofing material has been removed, you discover parts of the sheathing are deteriorated you need replace only the damaged sections.

Removing Roll Roofing

Any composition roll roofing, hot asphalt, or tar-mopped layers of roofing paper are removed in this manner:

1 • Slit the old roofing at one edge of the roof with a roofing knife.

2 • Slide any prying tool, such as a crowbar or shingle ripper, under the roofing material and pull the roofing material away from the sheathing.

Removing Shingles or Shakes

1 • Pry up each shingle with a crowbar, prize, shingle ripper, or a flat-bladed trowel. You may be able to pull most asphalt shingles free with your hands.

2 • Be careful not to damage any flashing under the shingles or shakes, around chimneys, in valleys, or around dormers and skylights.

3 • Pull the underlayment away from the sheathing. The paper will tear readily and is not difficult to remove.

4 • Pull out or drive in all nails in the sheathing, unless the sheathing is to be discarded.

REMOVING FLASHING

Removing Valley Flashing

Valley flashing is used to cover the joint where two roof planes meet. If the flashing is metal, a strip or squares of metal are normally placed over a 36″-wide strip of roofing paper, which runs vertically over the joint. Composition paper flashing is made of two layers. The

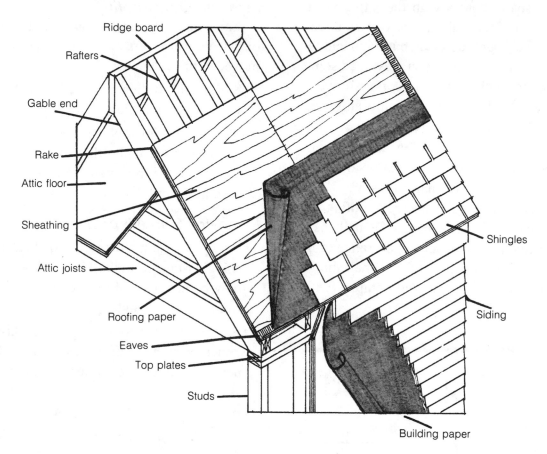

top layer is 36″ wide and has been cemented over an 18″-wide strip. Both layers are cemented to the drip edge at the eaves of the joint.

1 • Remove all of the nails visible in the flashing.

2 • Pry the flashing away from the roof.

3 • Save the flashing to be used as a pattern when you cut new flashing.

Removing Eaves Flashing and Drip Edges

Eaves flashing is a strip of roofing paper that is cemented over the metal drip edge. The drip edge is a strip of metal inserted between the edge flashing and the underlayment, used to shed water away from the roof and into the gutter, and it may have been secured with an occasional roofing nail.

1 • Pull the roofing paper away from the sheathing and expose the drip edge.

2 • Pull the nails out of the drip edge and remove the edge. Replacement drip edging is sold in strips and you will not need the old edging as a pattern.

Removing Chimney Flashing

1 • Remove all shingles from around the chimney.

2 • Pull all nails from the base flashing to the sheathing.

3 • Remove the cap flashing by prying each piece out of the mortar joints in the chimney.

4 • Pry off the base flashing.

Removing Vent Flashing

All flashing around vent pipes should be replaced as a matter of course, since you can do it with very little expense and almost no effort.

1 • Scrape away the roofing cement covering the flange at the base of the flashing.

2 • Pry out all nails in the flashing.

3 • Pull the flashing up and off the vent pipe.

Removing Dormers, Skylight, and Vertical Wall Flashing

All flashing found around the base of dormers, skylights, or between vertical walls and the edge of roofs, is attached to both the vertical members and the roof sheathing. To remove it, you may have to remove the wall covering.

1 • Remove enough of the wall covering to expose the flashing.

2 • Pry out all nails in the flashing and remove it.

REMOVING AND REPLACING SHEATHING

Damaged sheathing or boards should be replaced, but it is not necessary to discard all of the sheathing on a roof if it shows no signs of rot or weakness.

When replacing the boards in either open or closed sheathing, use boards of the same width. Plywood panels that are damaged need only have their deteriorated portions removed and then replaced with exterior-grade ply-

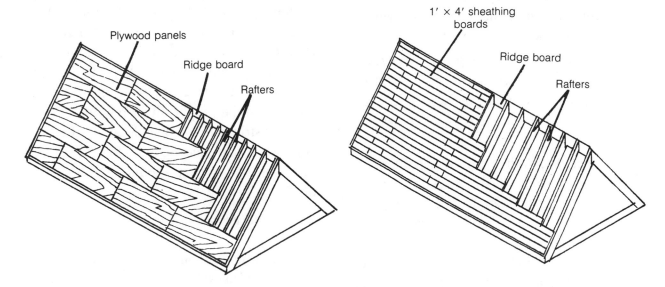

Replace only the deteriorated parts of the sheathing.

wood of the same thickness. When plywood is used as sheathing, it is nailed to the rafters, so the vertical seams between panels are over a framing member. When you are removing a section of a panel, cut it to fit exactly over the center of a rafter so that the new piece will be supported at each end by a rafter. To saw through the plywood over a rafter, set your circular power saw to the depth of the plywood thickness. When you inspect the sheathing for rot or damage, pay close attention to these areas of your roof:

• The hip and ridge boards may have incurred splits or decay. Replace them if they are in any way damaged.

• The gable (rake) edges may have split, decayed, or rotted. They should be replaced if they are in any way less than perfect.

• Fascia boards are nailed to the ends of the rafters as they overhang the walls of the house. The gutter is nailed directly to them and consequently they are exposed to considerable dampness that may cause them to rot. Replace them if they are bad.

• The sheathing along the edges of the eaves is also subjected to an inordinate amount of dampness and weight. If there is even a doubt about the solidness of the wood, replace it.

• Any decayed, split, or broken portions of the sheathing should be replaced. Note that the sheathing sometimes stops approximately ¾″ away from the chimney. It is supposed to, so that heat from the chimney will not cause it to burn. If you are replacing any sheathing around the chimney, maintain the same spacing between it and the mortar work as the old sheathing.

• Cover any open knotholes in sheathing with a piece of metal flashing nailed in place with galvanized roofing nails.

Installing a New Roof

Attaching Underlayment

When the sheathing is in order, you can attach 15-pound roofing paper (felt) to it, providing you are not installing wooden shakes or shingles. Wooden shakes and shingles should be attached to an open sheathing with no underlayment, so that air can circulate around the wood and prevent it from rotting. Any other roofing material should be applied over an underlayment of 15-pound asphalt-saturated roofing paper. If you have purchased roofing paper that has white lines on its outer side, you will not have to draw any chalk lines to guide you in putting down the shingles.

Underlayment is laid in horizontal strips beginning at the eaves and working up toward the peak of the roof, with each strip overlapping the strip below it by at least 2″. If a strip is too short and must be butted in the middle of its run, the overlap should be a minimum of 4″.

1 • Unroll about 4′ of the paper and align it with the eaves of the roof, and one rake (gable end). If one or both ends of the roof is a hip or valley allow a 6″ overlap beyond the centerline of the joint.

2 • Tack the paper in place using galvanized

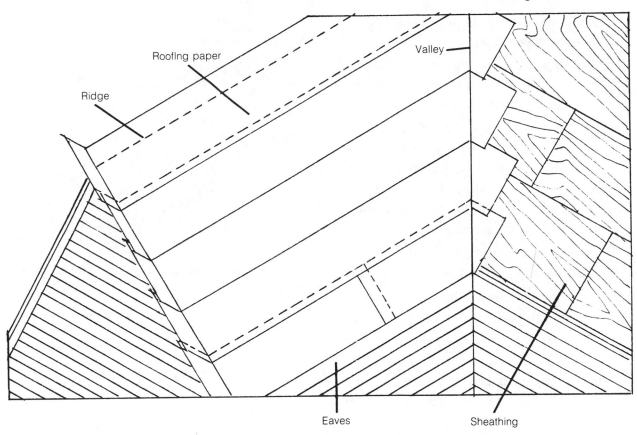

Ridge

Roofing paper

Valley

Eaves

Sheathing

Underlayment is usually 15-pound roofing paper laid in overlapping horizontal strips.

roofing nails placed 1″ in from the top edge of the paper and spaced every 2′. Be extremely careful that the paper is smooth and precisely in line with the eaves.

3 • Continue unwinding the paper and tacking it in alignment with the eaves until you reach the far end of the roof, or wherever it forms a hip or valley. Cut the paper with a knife or tin snips along the rake, or leave a 6″ overlap at hips or valley. If the paper large enough ends before you reach the end of the roof, overlap the next roll at least 4″. If you encounter a vent pipe, skylight, or chimney, cut a hole in the roofing paper for the obstacle.

4 • When you have covered the length of the roof and cut the underlayment, finish nailing it to the sheathing with roofing nails spaced 8″ apart and positioned 1″ inside the upper edge of the paper.

5 • There are several chalk lines on the roofing paper, which, if you have perfectly aligned the bottom edge of the paper with the eaves edge, will indicate a series of straight lines running the length of the roof. One of the chalk lines is 2″ from the top edge of the paper. To begin the second course of paper, start at the same gable end of the roof and unwind 4′ of paper. Carefully align the bottom edge

of the paper with the top chalk line and tack the paper in place.

Continue aligning the second course of paper with the chalk line on the first course, and then nail the paper in place.

6•Repeat laying paper, overlapping each course 2″ over the top of the course below it and leaving a 6″ overlap at the centerline of each hip or valley. Continue laying courses of paper until the top course is within 28″ of the ridgepole.

7•To cover the ridgepole, place the roll of paper on the ridge and unwind it.

8•Fold the paper over the ridge so that it overlaps the peak of the roof by at least 6″.

9•Align the bottom edge of the paper with the 2″ chalk line along the top edge of the last course of paper, and tack the paper along the ridgepole and edge of its overlap.

10•Cover all planes of the roof by repeating steps 1–9. As you complete coverage of both hips and valleys, overlap the 6″ flaps and drive a single nail through them.

Attaching Drip Edges

Drip edges are sold as long strips of aluminum, galvanized steel, or copper sheet metal, and are nailed along all rakes and eaves edges. Use nails made of the same metal as the drip edge to prevent corrosion.

1•Measure the length of the eaves or rake to be covered.

2•Cut the drip edge to the proper length.

3•Position the drip edge along the eaves or rake and nail it with the roofing nails po-

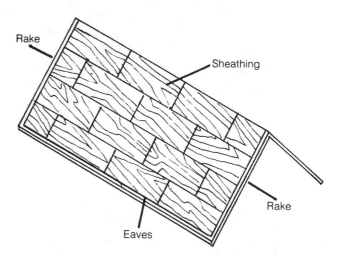

Metal drip edges must be placed along the rakes and eaves.

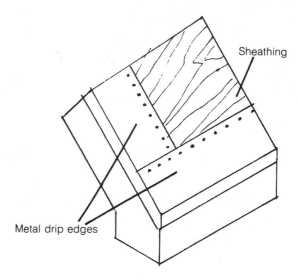

Metal drip edges must be placed along the rakes and eaves.

sitioned no closer to the edge than 1″ and spaced no more than 10″ apart.

4•At corners, where the drip edges meet, butt the two strips together and cover the joint with roofing cement.

5•The overlap should be bent over the edges of the roof, but need not be nailed.

INSTALLING FLASHING

Installing Eaves Flashing

The eaves and rakes must be given the added protection of a flashing strip, which overhangs the sheathing by ⅜″. The flashing can be either 65-pound or 90-pound mineral-surfaced roofing paper, but if you have a choice, use 90-pound paper. It will last longer. The paper must be soft and pliable when you install it so that is does not crack and lose its ability to shed water; if the flashing cracks as you are installing it, replace the damaged strip of paper.

If your house is in a locale that experiences moderate to heavy snowfall, the eaves flashing should be installed in double thickness; otherwise, a single thickness will suffice.

Installing Single-Thickness Eaves Flashing

1 • Measure and cut the flashing from a roll of 36″-wide 90-pound mineral-surfaced roofing paper.

2 • Lay the roofing paper along the eaves edge, extending it over the drip edge exactly ⅜″ along the eaves and at the rake (gable end). If one or both ends of the roof are a hip or valley, align one corner of the paper with the centerline and allow the other corner to overlap it. If the paper is too short for the roof run, make any side overlap at least 6″.

3 • Tack the roofing paper in place with roofing nails placed 1″ inside the top edge and 2′ apart.

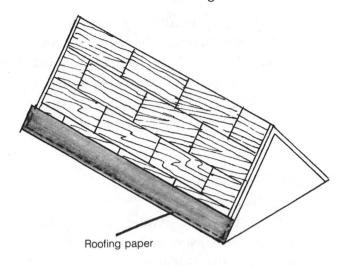

Roofing paper

Single-thickness eaves flashing.

4 • Using a straightedge and a knife, cut the end of the roofing paper overlapping valley or hip centerlines along the chalked centerline.

5 • Bend the ⅜″ overhang down against the drip edge along both the rake and eaves.

6 • Lift the ends and bottom edge of the roofing paper and apply a 6″-wide coating of roofing cement between the paper and the sheathing. Press the roofing paper in place over the edge.

7 • Nail the flashing along its bottom edge, spacing the roofing nails every 4″ and set 1″ back from the edge.

8 • One 36″-wide course of roofing paper is usually enough to place the top edge of the paper at least 12″ past the wall line of the house, if the roof pitch is $1/6$ or less. If the roof pitch is steeper than $1/6$, the eaves flashing would end 24″ inside the wall line, and you will probably need to overlap a

second course of roofing paper. The second course should have at least a 6″ overlap and is installed exactly as the first course. Nail the top edge of the second course to the sheathing; the bottom edge should be cemented with roofing cement and also be nailed.

Installing Double-Thickness Eaves Flashing

Double-thickness flashing on the eaves provides added insurance against dampness in areas where the annual snowfall is moderate to heavy. The strips of flashing are cut from 90-pound mineral-surfaced roll roofing and are attached to the sheathing in the same manner as single-thickness flashing, except that you must allow for a minimum of 19″ overlap. The flashing extends 12″ beyond the wall line (or 24″ if the roof pitch is $\frac{1}{6}$ or less).

1 • Cut a 19″-inch strip from 90-pound mineral-surfaced roofing paper.

2 • Install the strip, with its rough (mineral) surface down, along the eaves edge of the roof, extending it beyond the edge ⅜″, cementing and nailing it as is done with single-thickness flashing.

3 • Measure and cut a strip of 36″-wide flashing and install it with its smooth side down, over the 19″ strip, as with single-thickness flashing. If you need to overlap a second 36″ strip to bring the top of the flashing to 12″ or 24″ past the wall line, overlap the second strip at least 19″.

Installing Valley Flashing

Although valley flashing can be con-

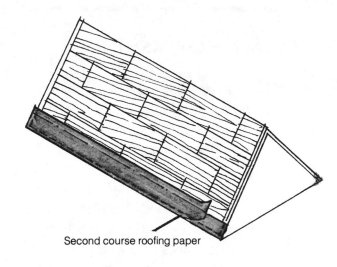

Second course roofing paper

Double-thickness eaves flashing.

structed from layers of 90-pound mineral-surfaced roofing paper, most professionals recommend metal flashing in all valleys, no matter whether the valley is to be open or closed. Your working time can be reduced considerably if you have preserved the old flashing and can use it as a pattern for cutting the new metal. You can use aluminum, galvanized steel, or copper sheet metal, which is preferably long enough to reach the entire length of the valley. The strip must extend at least 7″ on either side of the valley if the pitch is more than ½, and 10″ on each side if the pitch is less than ½. Whatever metal you choose, it must be installed over a 36″-wide strip of 30- or 65-pound roll roofing paper.

1 • Measure the length of the valley centerline, and add 30″ to allow for the V cuts to be made at its top and bottom.

2 • If you have saved the old flashing, use it as a cutting pattern. If the flashing cannot be used, lay the roofing paper out and use its

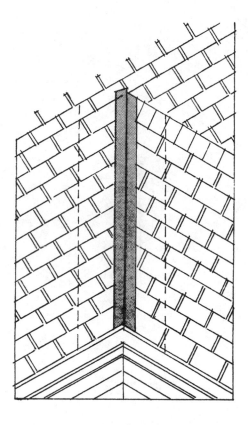

Open valley flashing.

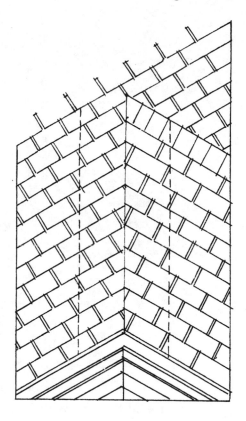

Closed valley flashing.

center (18″) to mark the Vs at both ends, then cut out the three triangles using a straightedge and knife. Be sure to allow an extra ⅜″ overhang at the bottom end to cover the drip edge. (Illustration B)

3 • Align the center of the roofing paper with the centerline of the valley and position the paper with the bottom edge of the V so that it overhangs the eaves by ⅜″. Align the top edge with the ridges of the intersecting roofs.

4 • Apply a 2″ wide application of roofing cement to the undersides of the bottom edge of the V and carefully align and press the V against the roof drip edges.

5 • Nail the sides of the roofing paper to the sheathing, spacing your nails 12″ apart and 1″ from the edges of the paper.

6 • Measure, cut, bend, and place the metal flashing in the valley. (Illustration C) The turned-down edges of the metal should fold over the drip edge. You can nail it in place using nails made of the same material as the flashing, but place them no more than ½″ inside the edges. Or you can space brackets every 8″ along the edges and nail them to the sheathing so they overlap the flashing. If the metal is not long enough for the valley, overlap the extra pieces by at least 4″.

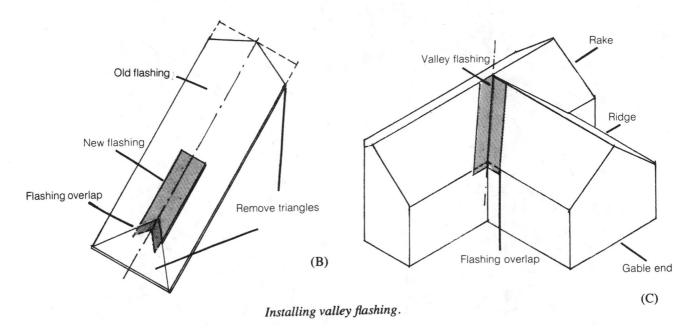

(B)

(C)

Installing valley flashing.

7 • If you intend to have an open valley, it is helpful if the metal flashing is marked on both sides with chalk lines that tell you where to stop each course of shingles. To make the chalk lines, measure 3″ from each side of the centerline at the top of the valley. Measure 4″ from each side of the bottom of the centerline. Stretch your chalk line between marks and snap two lines. (Illustration D)

Installing Flashing Between Roofs and Vertical Walls

If you are applying flashing around the intersecting planes of a dormer, where the roof of the dormer meets the roof of the house, you are working with a valley; around the base of the sides and front of the dormer, you are attaching flashing to vertical walls and the

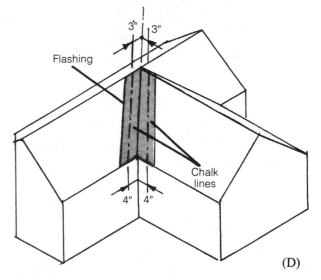

(D)

roof. Similarly, if your roof touches a wall of the house, the flashing is installed in the same manner.

The flashing between roofs and vertical walls can be metal or 65- or 90-pound roofing paper. If the siding on the vertical wall permits, slide the flashing up at least 4″ beneath it. If the siding is such that flashing cannot be placed under it, butt the flashing against the vertical wall and seal the joint with roofing cement. In both cases, the flashing overlaps the roof shingles that abut the wall.

Installing Roof Flashing on a Wall with Siding

1 • Measure the length of the roof that touches the vertical wall from the eaves to the ridge.

2 • Fold the flashing so that at least 4″ can be pushed up under the siding on the wall. One of the easiest ways of folding the flashing strip is to place a block of wood along its fold line and bend it up against the wood.

3 • The flashing strips are best applied as the roofing material is being placed, and it is easiest to apply if you cut the strips into overlapping pieces. To determine how many pieces you will need, divide the width of the roof by the length of each shingle exposure. Thus, if the roof is 100″ long and the exposure of each shingle is 5″, divide 5″ into 100″. You will need 20 flashing strips which should be cut and folded before you begin laying the shingles.

4 • As each course of shingles reaches the wall, beginning at the eaves, slide the first flashing strip up under the wall siding.

5 • Coat the underside of the flashing with asphalt roofing cement. Align the horizontal edge of the flashing with the exposure of the shingle, allowing it to be 1″ higher than

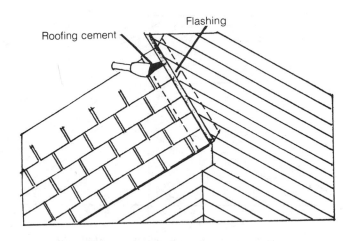

Installing roof flashing on a wall with siding.

the top edge of the exposed portion of the shingle. Press the flashing down on the end of the shingle.

Installing Roof Flashing on a Wall without Siding

1 • Cut an 8″ strip of 90-pound mineral-coated roofing paper equal to the length of the roof along the wall.

2 • Coat the underside of the paper flashing with asphalt roofing cement.

3 • Position the flashing strip on the roof, aligning it with the drip edge, and press it against the wall.

4 • Nail the strip to the sheathing with roofing nails spaced 4″ apart.

5 • Coat the paper flashing with asphalt roofing cement and cover it with the last shingle in each course. Do not drive any shingle nails through the flashing.

6 • When the shingles have all been laid, apply

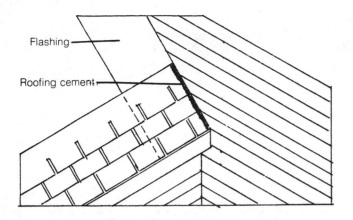

Installing roof flashing on a wall without siding.

a bead of roofing cement along the top edge of the flashing and the vertical wall.

Installing Chimney and Ventilator Flashing

Chimney flashing is applied while the shingles are being placed on the roof, as are the boots placed over the base of all vent pipes. Bring the shingle courses up to the base of the chimney or vent pipe, then install the flashing so that the lowest portion of it lays on top of the shingles. The side and top portions of the flashing is attached directly to the roofing paper, over the sheathing, and is covered by successive courses of shingles. (See Chapter 3 for procedures for installing chimney and vent pipe flashings.)

INSTALLING ROOF VENTS

When the temperature outdoors is 95°F, the air under the peak of your roof is 140°F. Since warm air rises above cooler air, when it gets to the peak of your attic it will remain there unless you provide adequate ventilation in the roof to allow the warm air to escape outside. There should be soffit vents installed along the underside of the roof overhang (soffit), which are merely gratings made of metal or plastic installed in holes cut to size in the soffit boards. With soffit vents your attic will receive a contact flow of outside air passing over the attic floor, but this flow will do nothing to lower the temperature of the attic if soffit vents are the only ventilation you have. Gable end vents can help, but far more efficient are roof vents. You can install several small vents along the ridge, or one or two larger powered vents. The powered vents should be thermostatically controlled so that the fan motor will go on as soon as the temperature under the roof reaches about 100°F, and shut off when it drops to around 85°F. Most roof vents are sold with a statement printed on their boxes that tells you how much floor space the vent can handle. Thus, if you measure the length times the width of your attic space and reach a number of square feet that is less than the rating of the roof vent, you can install it and be sure that not only will it keep your attic cool, it will also reduce the amount of energy needed by your air conditioner to keep the entire house comfortable during the hot summer months. All roof vents are installed in the same manner as chimney and vent pipe flashing (see Chapter 3).

1• Temporarily position the vent or vents on the back side of your roof as close to the

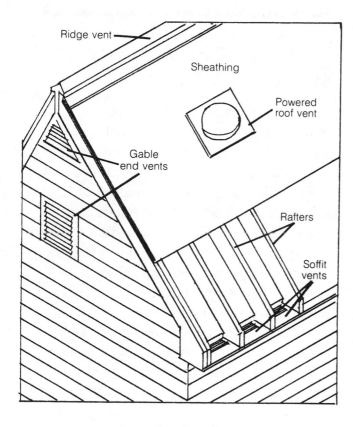

Types of roof ventilators.

peak as you can so they are not visible from the front of the house. (Illustration E) You do not have to put them on the back side of the roof, but they are a little unsightly by many people's standards. On a flat roof, a powered roof vent should be placed as close to the center of the roof as possible.

2•Measure the position of the unit from the gable ends, chimney, or any other marker that can be used inside the attic.

3•From inside the attic, using the marker as a guide, reposition the vent between rafters, and drill a hole up through the shea-

thing to mark the center of the hole you will cut for the vent. (Illustration F)

4•Go back up on the roof. Draw a circle on the roofing paper, using the hole drilled though the sheathing as the center. The diameter of the circle should be whatever size the vent manufacturer has designated in the instructions that come with the vent. (Illustration G)

5•Using a saber saw, cut the circle out of the sheathing.

6•Tack the flanges of the vent to the sheathing using roofing nails, to keep the vent in place until you are laying shingles around the ventilator.

7•Lay shingles up to the top of the bottom flange of the ventilator, sliding the top course under the bottom flange.

8•Coat the underside of the bottom flange with roofing cement and press it down over the shingles.

9•Nail the side flanges to the sheathing and cover each nailhead with roofing cement.

10•Bring each succeeding course of shingles up to the base of the ventilator, covering the side and top flanges.

11•Apply a bead of asphalt roofing cement to the edges of the shingles along the sides of the ventilator.

12•If the ventilator has a powered fan, make the appropriate electrical connections to the house wiring system.

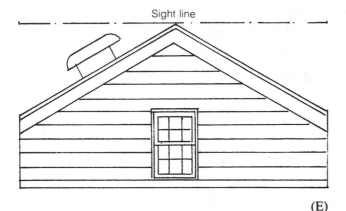

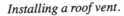

(E)

Installing a roof vent.

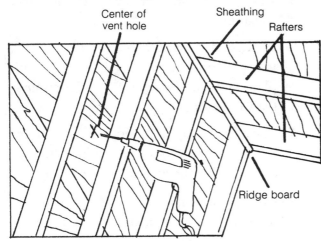

(F)

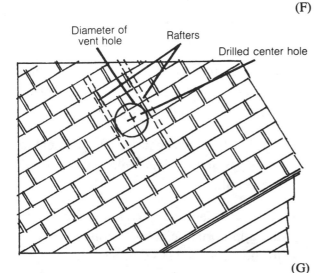

(G)

INSTALLING AN ASPHALT SHINGLE ROOF

Probably the most popular roofing material in use today is asphalt strip shingles. These are available in a variety of patterns, including a three-tab square butt, as well as two- and three-tab hex strips. You can also purchase asphalt in oversized single shingle versions.

Tools and materials • Tools needed for installing asphalt shingles include a hooked roofing knife, a hammer, a putty knife, a 2″ brush for applying roof cement, a folding rule, chalk line, and scaffolding.

Materials include 15- and 90-pound asphalt roofing paper, 1¾″ galvanized roofing nails, roofing cement, regular shingles, and a supply of preformed hip and ridge asphalt shingles.

The Starter Course: Roll Roofing Paper

The starter course is laid along the eaves edge, underneath the first course of shingles and over the underlayment. It can be either 90-pound roll roofing or shingles.

1 • Measure the length of the eaves edge.

2 • Unwind enough roll roofing to cover the eaves edge plus ¾″ and cut it into a strip 12″ wide.

3 • Place the roll roofing along the eaves, allowing it to extend ⅜″ over the rake and the eaves edge. The mineral-coated side of the roofing paper must face down, against the sheathing. If an end of the starter paper ends at a vertical wall or a valley, apply a 6″

strip of roofing cement to the flashing, as far as the valley chalk line or wall. Press the starter paper down on the cement.

4 • Nail the starter course with nails spaced every 8″ and 1″ inside the top edge of the paper.

The Starter Course: Shingles

1 • Cut a shingle in half or thirds and place it upside down at the edge of the roof so that it extends over the rake and eaves edge by ⅜″ and the tab edge points toward the peak of the roof.

2 • Nail the shingle with three roofing nails, one at each edge and one in the center of the strip. All nails should be placed high enough on the shingle so that they will be covered by the next course of shingles.

3 • Continue laying the starter course, using full shingles, placed so that their tabs point toward the roof peak, and attached with four nails evenly spaced across the upper third of the shingles, so that they will be covered by the tabs on the first course of shingles.

4 • The last two shingles in the starter course must be at least 6″ wide. Trim one or both of them accordingly. If the last shingle ends at a rake or a hip, it should overhang the roof edge by no more than ⅜″.

If the last shingle ends at a valley, trim it so that it will end along the chalk line. Coat the valley flashing with asphalt roofing cement and press the shingle down on the cement. Do not drive roofing nails into the

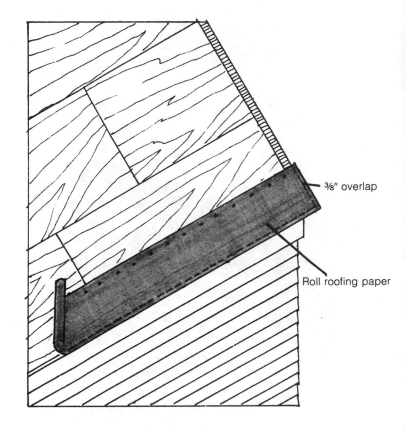

⅜″ overlap

Roll roofing paper

A starter course of roll roofing.

flashing; keep your nails on the sheathing side of the flashing.

5 • Cover all nailheads with daubs of roofing cement.

The First Full Course

The first full course of shingles is laid directly over the starter course with its mineral surface up and the tabs pointed down, toward the eaves edge.

1 • Align the first shingle with the bottom edge of the starter course and the ⅜″ overhang of the starter course at the rake.

2 • Nail the first shingle with six nails: two

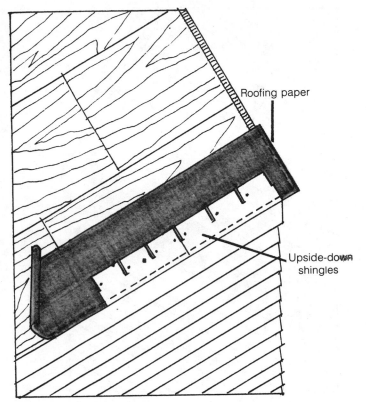

A starter course of shingles.

nails should be placed on either side of the slots between the tabs and one nail is placed 1″ from each side.

3 • Continue laying shingles in the course. The shingle strips are butted next to each other and aligned over the starter course. Each shingle is nailed with six roofing nails, like the first shingle.

4 • If the course ends at a rake edge, cut the last two shingles to fit over the final shingle in the starter course. Neither shingle should be less than 6″ wide.

If the course ends at a valley, coat the last 6″ or 8″ of the starter course with roofing cement and press the last shingle down on the cement. Nail the last shingle to the sheathing, not through the valley flashing.

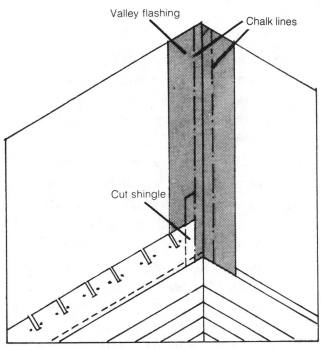

The last shingle in a starter course ending at a valley should be trimmed to meet the chalk line.

Installing the Second and Following Courses

Every other course of shingles must begin with a partial shingle so that the tab slots in adjacent courses are never aligned. You must also be careful that each course is in a straight line across the roof. When the first course of shingles has been laid over the starter course, all other courses are installed in this manner:

1 · Place the first shingle of the second course so that the slots between its tabs are over the center of the tabs in the first shingle in the first course. About a third of the shingle will hang beyond the rake of the roof. Cut off the overhang with a roofing knife.

2 · Align the cut shingle with the gable end of the roof so that it extends ⅜″ over the rake. Most asphalt roofing shingles have two colors. The tabs will be a different color than the top portion of the shingle strip. Only the tabs should be visible; the shingle is aligned with the color line in the first course of shingles. Or, if there is a chalk line on the roofing paper above the first course, line the top edge of the second course of shingles along that.

3 · All shingles are nailed in the same way, using six roofing nails. Each nail is located .5⅝″ above the butt edge of the shingle strip; that is, the bottom of its tabs. The two end nails are placed 1″ inside the side edges. One nail is placed on either side of the two slots 1½″ from the slot. It would add hours to your working time if you measured the position of each nail, but after you have nailed a course or two of shingles, you will develop a pretty good

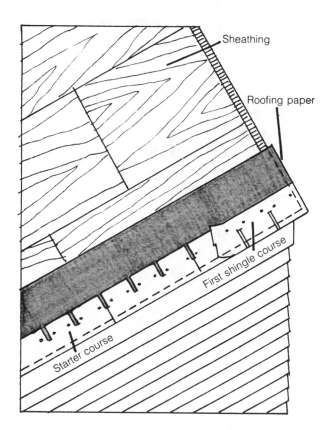

The first full course of shingles.

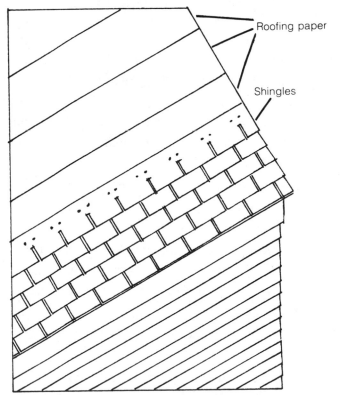

Positioning the second and subsequent courses of shingles.

feel for where the nails should be positioned. The important element to remember is that the nails must be covered by the course above the shingles you are attaching. So keep them all well inside the area between the top edge of the shingles and the top of the slots.

4 • End each course by trimming the last two shingles so that they are both at least 6″ wide. If the roof ends at a rake or hip, trim the last shingle to end ⅜″ beyond the edge. End the last shingle at the chalk line in any valleys.

Shingling Around and Over Flashing

The flashing along vertical walls, around the base of dormers, chimneys, ventilators, skylights, and vent pipes must be installed after the highest course of shingles has reached the bottom of the obstacle. The lower flange or bottom of the flashing is then nailed to the sheathing. Observe these rules when shingling around any obstacle that is protected by flashing:

1 • Cut the shingles in each course to fit around the contours of the obstacle, if necessary.

2 • Nail the shingles attendant to the flashing into the sheathing, not through the flashing. If you drive a nail through the flashing, cover the nailhead with roofing cement.

3 • Apply a 6″- to 8″-wide strip of asphalt roofing cement to the flashing and cover it with successive courses of shingles.

4 • When you have aligned the end shingles in each course with the chalk lines in valley flashing (see page 83), apply a bead of asphalt roofing cement along the shingle line, where the shingles meet at a closed valley or where they end over the flashing in open valleys.

Installing Hips and Ridges

Hips and ridge shingles are curved, measure 9″ × 12″, and have no tabs. You can purchase them wherever you buy your other roofing materials, but you can also use 90-pound mineral-surfaced roofing paper or strip shingles cut to the same 9″ × 12″ dimensions. If you cut your own hip and ridge shingles, bend them carefully along the 12″ centerline.

1 • The first hip or ridge shingle laid will have to be trimmed to fit at the lower end of the hip. (Illustration H)

2 • Apply a thin coat of asphalt roofing cement to the ridge or hip and place the first shingle along its 12″ centerline over the center of the ridge. (Illustration I)

3 • Fold the shingle over both sides of the ridge and secure it with two nails on each side. The nails should be 1″ from the sides and 5½″ from the top edge of the shingle. (Illustration J)

4 • Coat the ridge with roofing cement.

5 • Center the second shingle over the first with a 6″ overlap and nail it as described in step 3.

6 • Each successive shingle is positioned and nailed in the same way and overlaps the preceding strip by 6″.

7 • The last shingle, of necessity, has its four nails exposed. Cover the nailheads with daubs of asphalt roofing cement.

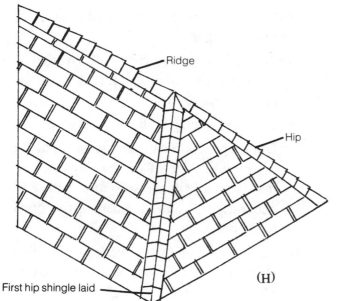

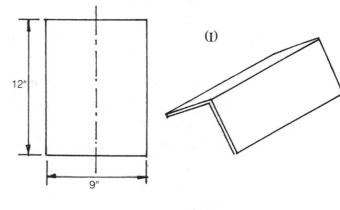

(I)

Installing hip or ridge shingles.

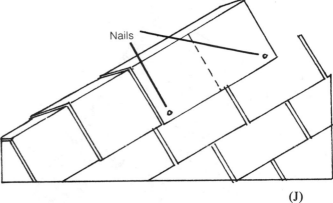

Installing Roll Roofing on a Flat Roof

ROLL ROOFING IS COMPOSED of mineral-surfaced composition roll roofing, known as 90-pound roofing paper. The paper can be installed horizontally or vertically, and the nails can be hidden or exposed. As a rule, if the roof pitch is $^7/_{12}$, the strips should be installed horizontally. Any roof with a lower pitch than $^7/_{12}$ is easier to cover if the strips are

vertical. The roof should be prepared in the same manner as a roof being shingled, except there is no need to install 15-pound roll roofing underlayment or flashing roll strips along the eaves. The procedure for installing roll roofing vertically or horizontally is essentially the same:

1• After the roof has been fully prepared, measure the width of the roof from rake to rake.

2• Unroll the measured length of roofing

paper plus 1½" to provide ¾" at each rake to be folded over the edges.

3 • Cut the roofing paper with a roofing knife. Allow the roofing paper to be warmed by the sun to make it pliable without cracking.

4 • Place the first strip along the eaves edge, extending it ¾" over the eaves edge and each of the gable ends.

5 • Nail the top edge of the strip, spacing your nails every 18". Nails along the ends and the bottom edge should be spaced every 2" and 1" in from the edges.

6 • Measure and cut the second strip of roofing paper.

7 • Place the second strip with a 6" overlap on the first strip, and extend it ¾" beyond the rake edges.

8 • Nail the top edge of the second strip.

9 • Draw a pencil line on the first strip, along the bottom edge of the second strip, so that you can lift the strip and paint a 6" wide stripe of roofing cement on the top of the first strip.

10 • Press the second strip overlap on the first strip and nail the sides and bottom edge, placing your nails every 2".

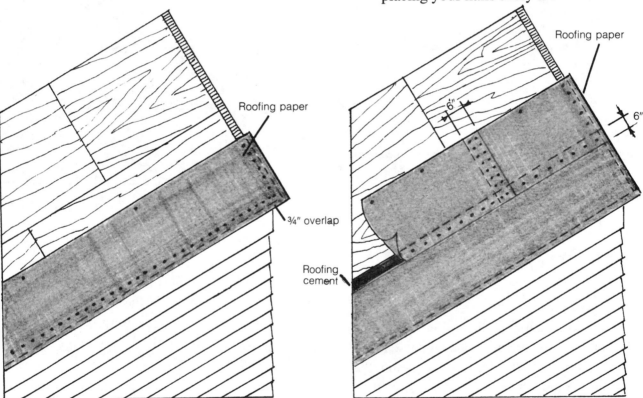

Laying the first course of roll roofing.

Laying the second and subsequent courses of roll roofing.

11• Continue laying each successive strip following steps 1–10. If it is necessary to use more than one piece to complete a horizontal run, overlap the pieces at least 6″ and seal the overlap with roofing cement, then nail the overlap with two parallel rows of nails.

Covering Valleys with Roll Roofing

1• Snap a chalk line down the center of the valley flashing.

2• Trim each strip to fit along the chalk line.

3• When all of the strips have been installed, coat the joint seam with roofing cement.

Covering Hips and Ridges

1• Trim each strip so that it will extend 4″ over the hip or ridge.

2• Install the strip and bend the 4″ overlap over the hip or ridge line. Nail the flap every 4″, 1″ in from the end of the strip.

Covering Ridges

1• The last strip of roll roofing on the roof should be trimmed to extend beyond the ridge by 4″.

2• Position the strip with a 6″ overlap on the course below it and nail it in place.

3• Bend the extra 4″ over the ridge and nail the strip to the sheathing with nails placed every 8″ and 1″ in from the edge.

Finishing the Edges, Hips, and Ridges

1• Bend the ¾″ overhang of each strip at the rakes, and nail the paper every 6″.

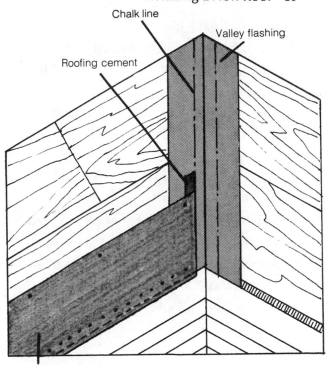

Roll roofing should cover valley flashing to the chalk line.

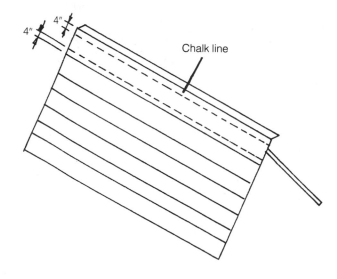

Hips and ridges are covered by roll roofing.

2 • Measure and cut strips of half-round molding to fit against the eaves edges under the roofing paper. Nail the strips along the eaves.

3 • Fold the roofing paper overhanging the eaves and nail it to the molding at 6″ intervals.

4 • Cover all nails exposed along the edges with roofing cement.

5 • Cut 12″-wide strips of roofing paper to fit over the full length of each hip or ridge.

6 • Apply a 2″-wide strip of roofing cement on each side of the hip or ridge.

7 • Position the cap strip over the ridge or hip and press it in place.

8 • Nail the strip on both sides of the hip or ridge, spacing nails 2″ apart and 1″ in from the edges of the paper.

9 • Cover all nailheads with asphalt roofing cement.

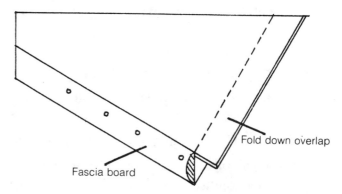

The edges of hips and ridges are finished with roll roofing attached to a curved molding.

chapter 5

REPAIRING EXTERIOR SIDING

THE OUTSIDE WALLS OF a wooden house are constructed by first erecting a system of studs precisely spaced every 16″ on center (o.c.). The studs, like the rafters supporting the roof, are then covered with sheathing, which may be 1″ × 6″ boards, exterior-grade plywood, fiberboard, or gypsumboard. The thickness of the sheathing material is normally between $^5/_{16}$″ and ½″ and is covered with weatherproof building paper (felt), which forms a moisture barrier between the inside of the house and the exterior siding material. The only variation in this construction is when the exterior wall is to be made of brick, stone, or concrete, in which case the outside wall is usually erected and the wooden framing members are then assembled against the inside of the wall, or a second wall is erected, leaving approximately an 8″ space between the masonry work and the second wall. In many older masonry houses plaster is then attached to the inside wall without the use of wooden framing.

TYPES OF SIDING

Siding, like roofing materials, is sold by the square, which is defined as 100 square feet, or a 10′ × 10′ area. There are seven types of siding:

Wooden clapboard, shingles, shakes• Clapboard is milled in numerous configura-

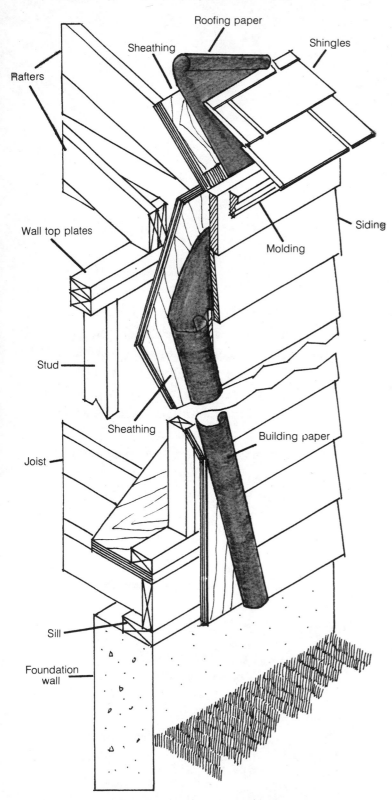

Rafters

Roofing paper

Sheathing

Shingles

Wall top plates

Siding

Molding

Stud

Sheathing

Building paper

Joist

Sill

Foundation wall

Anatomy of the side of a house and its roof.

tions, all of which are shaped boards that are generally thinner along one edge. Shakes and shingles used on the sides of houses are the same as those placed on roofs. Wood is perhaps the most common siding material because it is easy to shape and install. But all wooden siding requires occasional maintenance and repair, although with proper upkeep it should last the lifetime of the house.

Hardboard • A dense, waterproof version of hardboard is available in designs that resemble shingles, shakes, and clapboard. While hardboard looks like wood, it has the advantage of not cracking and therefore requires less maintenance.

Asbestos • You can purchase asbestos as shingles or in sheets that look exactly like stucco. In either version the asbestos is brittle and must be handled carefully during installation. It is, however, fireproof and relatively inexpensive.

Plastic • Polyvinylchloride (PVC) is manufactured to resemble the other types of siding and is available in a range of colors and textures. It is fire-resistant, will endure years of weathering but its color may fade with time.

Stucco • This is actually cement that is applied to the sides of a building in three thin layers. It offers all of the advantages of concrete, and is waterproof, fire-resistant, and extremely durable. (See Chapter 7 for information concerning stucco and its repairs.)

Aluminum • Aluminum siding is shaped into sheets that look like clapboard and comes in a variety of baked-on colors and styles. Some versions require repainting occasionally, but otherwise aluminum is very near maintenance free. About its only disadvantage is that it can be dented with relative ease.

Galvanized steel • Steel is the wave of the future. It is stronger than aluminum, is shaped to resemble clapboard and other siding styles, is tough, and will not dent. It is sold with several different colors baked on its exterior surface and can be purchased with an insulation backing that offers a good R-value. It too is maintenance free and usually comes with a 20-year guarantee.

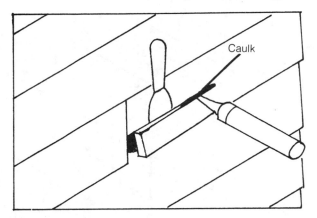

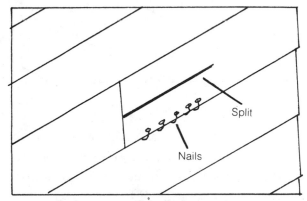

After caulking a split in clapboard you can hold the pieces together by driving nails under the bottom edge of the board.

REPAIRS TO SIDING

Both hardboard and plastic siding are applied in sheets, and whenever any damage occurs to them the best way of effecting repairs is to replace the entire sheet. Steel almost never has anything go wrong with it, but if something should happen it too must be replaced in sections. Wooden shakes, shingles, and clapboard require the most repairs of any siding types, while damage to stucco, asbestos, and aluminum is minimal, with only an occasional repair ever having to be made.

Tools and materials • No matter what material your siding is made of, the tools you will need to make repairs include a claw hammer, shingle ripper (nail puller), backsaw, chisel, hacksaw, pliers, crowbar (preferably one with a wide, thin blade.) Materials necessary are galvanized roofing nails, roofing cement, caulking, building paper.

Clapboard Repairs

If the boards in a clapboard siding have developed minor cracks, you can fill the fissures with caulking compound or wood putty and then paint over the repair. Clean the entire area around the crack with a wire brush before applying the caulking, and smooth the repair material carefully to present an even exterior surface.

Replacing Clapboard

Badly cracked, rotted, or split clapboard should be replaced with new boards that are milled to the same design as the rest of the siding. You may need to take a piece of the old siding with you when you purchase the replacement clapboard, to be sure they are identical.

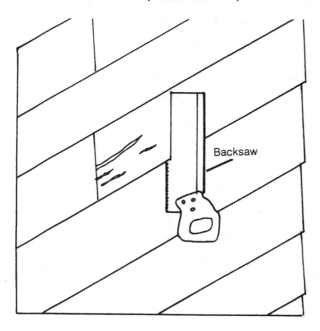

Replacing clapboard.   (A)

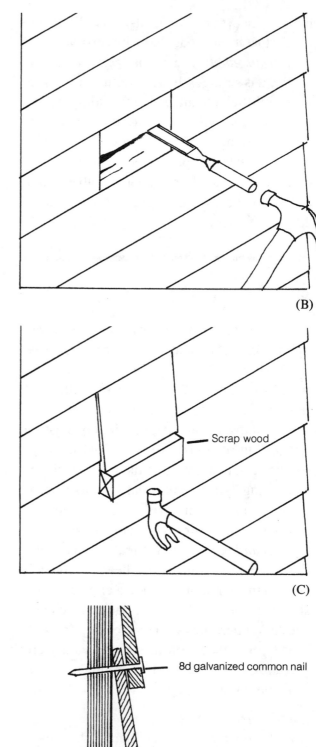

1 • Cut out the damaged area with a small handsaw. If you need room for your saw, insert wedges under the board to hold it away from the wall. (Illustration A)

2 • When both ends of the bad section are cut, push the wedges a little higher under the board.

3 • Knock the damaged piece free with a chisel and hammer. (Illustration B) If part of the board remains under the course above it, use a hacksaw blade to cut the nails. When the entire section has been removed, depress the course over the hole and pull the nails out with a claw hammer, a nail puller, or pliers.

4 • If the exposed building paper is torn, coat it with roofing cement or place a new piece of 15-pound felt over the tear. Nail the patch with galvanized roofing nails. Seal its edges and nailheads with caulking.

5 • Measure and cut a new length of clapboard.

6 • Slide the new piece under the course and gently tap it in place. Hold a block of wood against the butt edge of the patch so it is not dented. (Illustration C)

7 • Nail the new section in place at its top and bottom edges with 8d. galvanized finishing nails. (Illustration D) Countersink all nailheads and cover them with wood putty. Fill all joints with caulking where the patch meets the rest of the siding.

8 • Prime the patched area and apply a finish paint.

above the shingle or shake you have removed. (Illustration F)

4 • Slide a new piece into the hole.

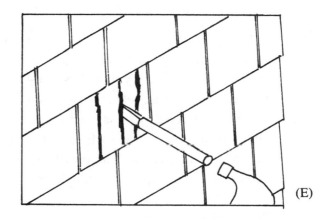

(E)

Repairing siding of wood shingles and shakes.

Repairing Wood Shingles and Shakes

Any nails that have popped in wood shingles or shakes can simply be driven in again. If any refuse to take hold, pull the old nail and drive a slightly large diameter nail through the same hole.

If a shingle or shake is cracked but not broken, slide a piece of building paper under it and drive nails through each of the cracked pieces.

When a shake or shingle is in such bad shape that it must be replaced, do the following:

1 • Split the damaged shingle or shake into pieces by driving a chisel up through its bottom edge. (Illustration E)

2 • Pull the pieces free.

3 • Cut or pry out any nails left in the course

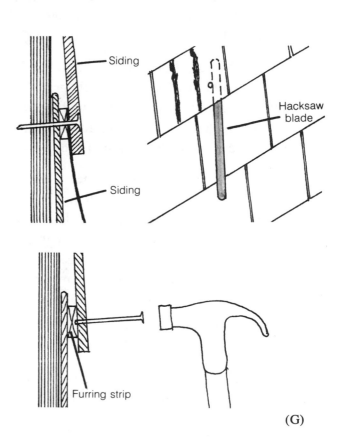

(G)

5 • Nail the new shingle in place, driving your nails through the course above it. Nails should be placed 1″ in from the edges of the shingle or shake. (Illustration G)

Fixing Asbestos Shingles

The most common repair to asbestos shingles is loose nails, which you can simply hammer in again. Be aware that asbestos is an extremely brittle material, so it is safer if you drive your nails almost to the surface of the shingle, then use a nailset so that your hammer has less chance of hitting the shingle and cracking it.

If nails are missing, drill new pilot holes an inch or two from the old nail holes. Drive annular ring galvanized steel nails into the shingles and fill the old holes with caulking.

If an asbestos shingle is cracked, but its pieces remain in place, pry each piece up enough to slide a piece of 15-pound roofing paper under the shingle. Drill pilot holes and drive new nails into the bottom of each piece.

If the shingle must be replaced, use a hammer and chisel to demolish it; do not damage any adjacent shingles. Slide a new shingle in place and drive nails through the predrilled holes along its bottom edge.

Should many shingles need to be replaced, rent a *shingle cutter,* which can reduce shingles to any size with relative ease. The cutter also has a lever punch for making pilot holes.

It is unlikely that new asbestos shingles will exactly match the color of the ones on your house. At best, you may be able to paint the replacement shingles to approximately match the rest. The easiest way of hiding repaired shingles is to paint the entire house.

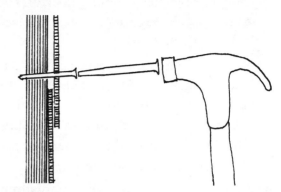

When hammering asbestos be careful not to crack the shingle.

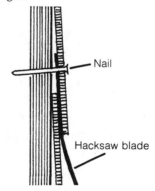

Nail

Hacksaw blade

Use a hacksaw blade or shingle ripper to cut or pry up nails in a cracked asbestos shingle.

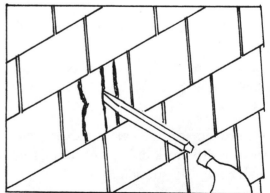

To remove a damaged asbestos shingle use a hammer and chisel.

Repairs to Aluminum Siding

Aluminum rarely needs to be repainted, but even a heavy hailstorm can dent the aluminum siding on your house. Fortunately, the dents can be removed easily:

1 • Place two or three washers around a small, self-tapping screw.

2 • Drive the screw into the center of the dent.

3 • Grip the washers around the screw head with a pair of pliers and pull until the dent flattens out.

4 • Remove the screw.

5 • Fill the screw hole with plastic aluminum and allow it to harden.

6 • File and/or sand the plastic aluminum smooth.

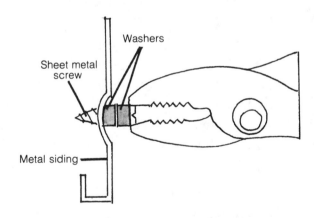

Pulling a dent out of aluminum siding.

Replacing Aluminum Siding

Occasionally, if it was not installed properly, aluminum siding may buckle under a hot summer heat, and need to be straightened or replaced. Here's how:

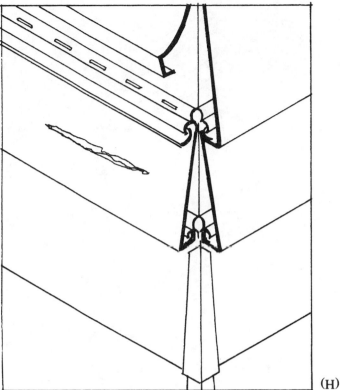

(H)

To replace damaged aluminum siding, first remove the corner caps.

1 • Remove the corner caps covering the joint at the end of the siding. (Illustration H)

2 • Pry up the overlapping course.

3 • Remove the nails in the top flange and both end flanges.

4 • Lift the panel off the side of the house. (With some aluminum panels you may have to remove all of the pieces above the damaged one, starting at the top of the wall and working down).

5 • Bend the warped panel until it is flat.

6 • Install the repaired piece or replacement panel, locking it over the flanges in the

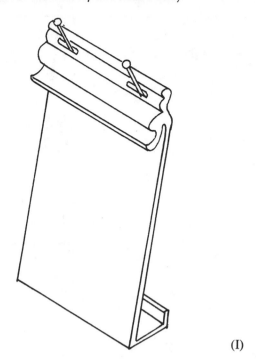

(I)

A replacement panel of aluminum siding.

existing siding, and nail it in place. (Illustration I)

7• Replace the corner caps.

Repairing Stucco

Stucco is applied in two or three layers, over a metal mesh nailed to the wall sheathing. The problem with stucco is that it is susceptible to cracking, and every crack is liable to let water work its way under the surface and cause ever-widening damage. The remedy is to repair any cracks you find in stucco as soon as you notice them.

The cracks can come from a number of natural causes that include uneven settlement of the house, or the difference in expansion and contraction rates between the stucco and whatever is underneath it. If the underpinning is wood, any break in the stucco can rot out the sheathing and cause a complicated repair that involves removing large areas of both stucco and the sheathing.

When repairing stucco follow these steps:

1• Scrape away all loose material in and around the damaged area, using a dull knife or chisel. (Illustration J)

2• Undercut the edges of the damaged spot so that the patch will be wider at its base than at the outside surface. The undercut helps the new stucco adhere.

3• If any of the wire mesh under the stucco has rusted, clip it out with tin snips.

4• Replace the wire mesh, nailing it to the sheathing.

5• Mix 1 part portland cement with 4 parts silica sand and add just enough water to make a puttylike consistency. When you are finished mixing, the mortar should be stiff enough to stand by itself on your trowel. (Illustration K)

6• Spray the damaged area with water.

7• Push the mortar into the webbing of the wire mesh, and fill the hole no more than halfway (you should see part of the mesh). (Illustration L) Scratch the surface of the stucco with a wire brush or the point of your trowel and allow the mortar to set, but not to dry completely.

8• Apply a second coat of mortar, almost filling the hole. Allow the mortar to dry for at least 12 hours.

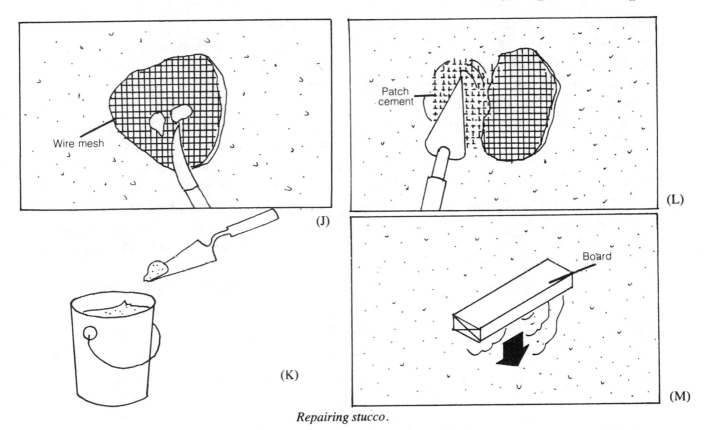

Repairing stucco.

9 • Apply a final coat of mortar to the hole, leveling it with the surrounding stucco surface. Smooth it off by pulling a board over the surface. (Illustration M)

10 • Texture the surface to match the surrounding stucco. Allow the mortar to dry for at least two days.

11 • Paint the stucco to match the surrounding surface.

Caulking

Caulking is about the easiest task you can take on in repairing the outside of your house. It is also boring, but absolutely necessary if you want your home to be energy efficient during the winter and keep insects and dirt out of it all year round. The caulking should last at least five years.

Caulking is used to fill the joints between any two materials on the outside of your house. You will find it between the trim and the siding at each corner, around the doors and windows, between the siding and the chimney, between steps and the side of the house, between the foundation and the siding, wherever a wing meets the main house, around water pipes and electrical conduits, everywhere.

You can purchase caulking in bulk (1- and 5-gallon cans), in squeeze tubes (for small jobs), and in cartridges used in caulking guns, which contain enough caulking to make a bead ¼″ in diameter 100′ long. Given double-hung windows measuring 2′ × 4′, you can expect to use one cartridge to caulk about four windows. Cartridges are without question the easiest form of caulking to use, but they can get to be expensive if you are recaulking a whole house. On the other hand, the bulk version is awkward since the barrel of the caulking gun must be cleaned before each reloading.

You will be confronted by a host of caulkings on the market, most of which fall into the categories listed below.

Procedure for Caulking

When you are caulking, plan to do your work on a day when the temperature is between 40° and 80°F. If you must caulk in temperatures that are above 80°F, place the caulking in the refrigerator for an hour or two before you use it and whenever you are taking a break. This will keep it from running. If you must work in temperatures below 40°F, you can warm the caulking by putting it in your oven, set to warm. Don't cook the cartridge; too much heat can make it break open—just warm it.

In an emergency, you can buy caulking in a

Type	Use	Requirements	Solvent	Comments
Oil-based	General caulking/glazing	Needs priming; must be painted	Turpentine; paint thinner	Shrinks; inexpensive
Polybutane cord	Wide or deep cracks	Does not adhere; press in place	None	Do not paint
Butyl	Metal-to-wood or metal-to-masonry joints	None	Paint thinner	Can be painted immediately
Neoprene	Cracks in concrete	Requirements vary from brand to brand	Toluene	Fumes
Silicone	Waterproof joints	Follow manufacturer's instructions	Paint thinner	Does not stick well to painted surfaces; costly; lasts 15–20 years
Oakum	Very wide or deep cracks	Must be forced	None	Cover with additional compound

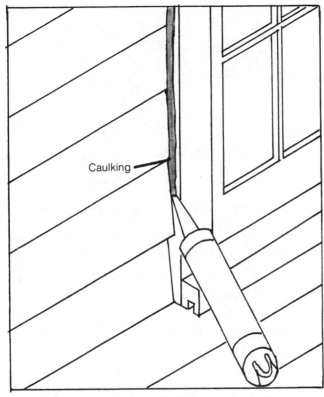

Caulking is applied from the highest point in the seam to the lowest.

rope form that is unrolled and forced into the seam with your fingers or a putty knife.

With many, but not all caulking, it is best to apply a coat of primer to the seam and then caulk. Then allow the caulking to set for several days before covering it with a final coat of paint.

No matter what the seam may be, and irrespective of the type of caulking you are using, the procedure for caulking is always the same:

1 • Thoroughly clean the seam, using a wire brush, scraper, or screwdriver.

2 • Wipe the seam absolutely clean with a rag dipped in turpentine, toluene, or paint thinner.

3 • Apply the caulking, working from the highest point in the seam down to the bottom.

4 • Smooth the bead of caulking if necessary with your finger or a putty knife.

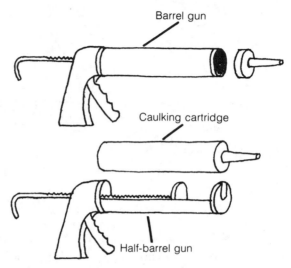

Full-barreled caulking guns are used with bulk compound. Half-barreled guns are for cartridges.

Using a Caulking Gun

Caulking guns are metal barrels that have a plunger at their back; the plunger is moved forward against the bottom of the caulking cartridge by pulling a trigger. There is nothing complicated about loading or using the gun, but there are some tricks to remember when you are caulking.

1 • Before loading the cartridge in the caulking gun, slice off the end of its spout at a 45° angle, using a sharp knife. (Illustration N)

2 • Push a nail into the hole in the end of the cartridge to break its inner seal. But leave the nail in place until you are ready to begin caulking.

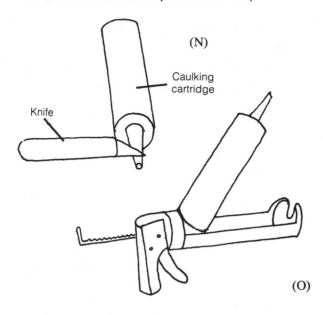

(N)

Caulking cartridge

Knife

(O)

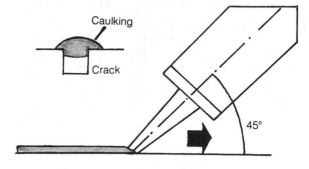

Caulking

Crack

45°

Working with a caulking gun. (P)

stop until you have filled the entire seam.

7 • When you have finished caulking, twist the gun lever and pull it back so that pressure on the bottom of the cartridge is released. If you do not take pressure off the cartridge, the caulking will tend to drip. You should also plug up the hole in the end of the tube with a large-headed nail.

3 • Pull the plunger handle all the way out, so that the plate it is attached to is at the back of the gun.

4 • Place the bottom of the cartridge against the back of the gun and lay the cartridge flat in the gun barrel. (Illustration O)

5 • When you begin caulking, rotate the gun lever so that the serrated side of the plunger handle is facing downward, toward the handle of the gun. Pull the trigger once to be sure it is advancing the lever against the bottom of the cartridge.

6 • Remove the nail from the end of the cartridge and place the angled end of the cartridge against the face of the seam and draw it slowly down the joint, holding the gun at a 45° angle to the seam. Pull the trigger of the gun whenever the caulking ceases to flow out of the cartridge; try to keep an even pressure on the gun trigger so that a steady, even bead of caulking comes out of the cartridge. If you can manage it, don't

Rope caulking

Rope caulkings can be used to fill wide seams.

chapter 6

PAINTING THE EXTERIOR OF YOUR HOUSE

ALUMINUM AND STEEL siding rarely, if ever, need painting, but exterior wooden siding must be protected from the weather every three to five years. You could hire a house-painter to do the chore, but that is liable to cost you upwards of a $1,000 plus the $9 to $11 for each gallon of paint. On the other hand, painting the outside of a house is not difficult labor and with enough hands (including adolescents) it can be done in relatively short order, once the exterior surfaces have been properly prepared.

Paints and Primers

Oil- or Water-based Paints?

The two types of paints used on house exteriors are oil-based or water-based (latex). *Oil-based paints* dry to a high gloss and are often thick enough to cover small imperfections, such as hairline cracks and dents. The bad news is that they must be thinned and cleaned with mineral spirits, benzene, or turpentine, and cleaning the brushes, or yourself, is not much fun.

Latex paints will not wash off your house when they are rained on; they will last just as long as oil-based paints. You can purchase water-based paints that work on masonry as well as wood and metal, and the great advantage of them all is that their solvent is water, so cleanup of yourself and the equipment is considerably easier than it is with oil-based paints.

Both base types can be used to cover exterior trim, masonry, metals, and decks (such

103

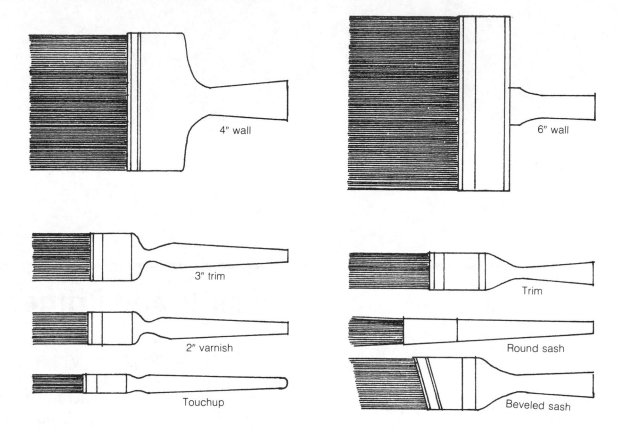

Paint brushes.

as porch floors). However, there are specifically formulated latex paints that dry to a flat finish for use on shakes and shingles, and water-soluble masonry paints made for painting stucco, brick, concrete, and cement blocks. These water-soluble masonry paints resist the alkali in masonry, which often causes other types of paint to streak. As for decks, the latex paints dry flatter than the oil-based deck paints and tend to present a less slippery surface when they have dried.

Exterior Primers

Anytime you scrape or sand off the paint on an exterior wall and expose the raw wood, you must give the area a coat of primer. Professionals in the paint industry strongly recommend an oil- or alkyd-based primer paint, which can soak into the wood fibers and help protect it from the elements. If you are painting metal, the recommendation is a rust-inhibiting alkyd or latex primer, rather than an oil-based. Masonry, because of its alkali content, should have a latex primer, which can inhibit alkali from discoloring the final coat of paint.

Once the primer has been applied, then the actual process of painting can begin.

Brushes, Rollers, and Paint Pads

BRUSHES

Before you use any new brush, hold it under running water and pull at it to remove all of its loose bristles.

Painting with Brushes

Grip a wide, heavy "beaver tail" brush as if it were a tennis racket. Long-handled sash and trim brushes are held as if they were a pencil. Chisel-edged beading brushes are held with your thumb on one side of the handle and your fingers on the other.

1 • Dip half the length of the bristles into the paint.
2 • Tap the metal ferrule that holds the bristles against the rim of the can to get rid of any excess paint. Do not draw the bristles across the rim of the can.
3 • Exert a minimum of pressure on the bristles as you pull them across the surface you are painting. Paint in one direction for a distance of about twice the length of the bristles, then brush back over your first stroke.
4 • Work in small areas, using short overlapping strokes.
5 • Start each new section two brush strokes away from a painted section, then work back to it.

Beading • Beading is done with a chisel-edged brush, whenever you have two colors meeting or are painting the mullions in windows. To bead: **1**) Dip the brush in paint and tap it against the can rim. **2**) Draw the bristles along the paint line, where the two colors meet, keeping them about $1/16''$ away from the edge so that the paint can spread enough to touch the line.

Cleaning Brushes

1 • Soak the brush in whatever solvent is used for the paint it was dipped in. Latex paints require warm water; oil-based and alkyd paints need turpentine, benzene, or paint thinner.
2 • Work the solvent between the bristles all the way up to the base of the handle. To do this you have to squeeze the bristles with your fingers.
3 • Rinse the bristles in the solvent and shake out excess solvent. You may have to do this several times until the brush comes clean.

Clean a paint brush by working solvent between the bristles.

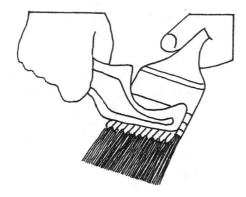

Combing the bristles of a brush with a brush comb helps it regain its pliability.

4 • Comb the bristles with a brush comb. This will straighten the bristles and also remove any stubborn paint.

5 • Wash the brush with warm water and soap.

Rejuvenating Old Brushes

An improperly cleaned brush will get stiff. Follow this procedure to make the bristles flexible again.

1 • Suspend the brush in a coffee can full of a commercial brush softener, turpentine, benzene, a paint thinner, or even paint remover.

2 • Scrape the bristles with a putty knife, then comb them with a brush comb.

3 • Soak the brush in solvent overnight.

4 • Wash away any remaining paint with a mixture of soap, one cup of turpentine, and a quart of water.

5 • Rinse in clean water and comb the bristles with a brush comb.

Storing Brushes

The weight of a stored brush must never rest on the bristles.

• You can drill a hole through the handle of any brush, then hang it on a wire hook.

• You can also wrap the brush in tin foil or heavy paper and hang it up or store it flat.

• If you drill a hole through the base of the brush handle and suspend it over a coffee can filled with solvent, by sliding a small rod through the hole and resting the rod on the rim of the can, you can soak the bristles in solvent without standing the brush on them.

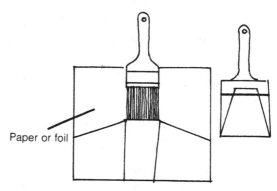

Paper or foil

Brushes may be stored wrapped in heavy paper (top), suspended in a can of solvent (bottom), or hung from a hook.

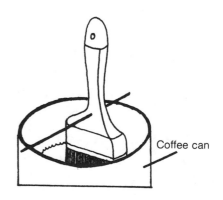

Coffee can

ROLLERS

Rollers are manufactured in a variety of sizes and shapes and can be used to cover trim or small areas, corners or whole walls. You can buy rollers with different naps for use with different paints. Lambswool is normally used with latex or alkyd paints; mohair is best with oil-based paints. Long-napped rollers are excellent on rough surfaces (masonry, brick, stucco); short naps are best on smooth surfaces. You will get more use out of your rollers if you use each one for a different paint type.

Using a Roller

1 • Pour paint in your paint pan and push the roller through it until the nap is completely covered. (Illustration A)

2 • Your first stroke should be about 3′ long and made by pushing the roller away from you. Make your second stroke without lifting the roller from the surface by bringing it back to you at a slight angle to make a zigzag. (Illustration B)

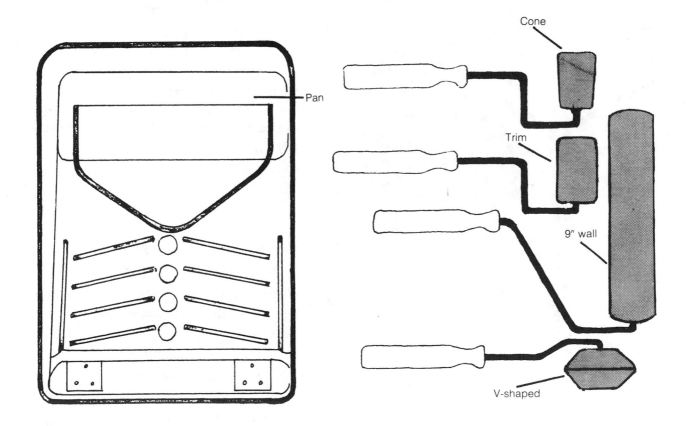

A roller pan and some of the roller shapes available.

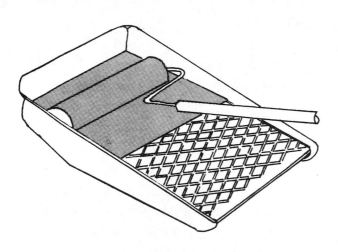

Working with a roller.　　(A)

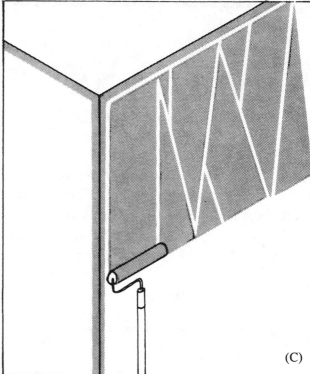

(C)

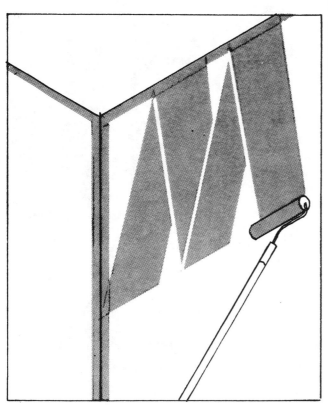

(B)

3 • Finish painting with zigzag strokes at right angles running to the first ones. (Illustration C)

4 • Go to the the next section and repeat steps 1–3.

Cleaning Rollers

1 • Roll all excess paint on a newspaper.

2 • Remove the roller from its handle.

3 • Clean the roller in whatever solvent is needed for the paint you used by gripping the roller and squeezing the nap until all of the paint is pushed out of it.

4 • Rinse in clear solvent and squeeze the roller until all of the solvent is removed.

5 • Stand the roller on end or hang it up to dry. Never lay a roller on its nap or it will become matted.

PAINT PADS

Many people contend that paint pads do an even smoother, faster job than rollers. Pads can be bought in 7″ and 9″ lengths as well as mini sizes for doing intricate work. Some of them have tiny wheels or tabs along one edge of their base plate that can be extended past the edge of the pad for cutting-in around woodwork.

You use a paint pad by dipping it in paint and then wiping the pad on the surface to be painted. The foam rubber leaves no brush strokes and will give you an even application of paint.

Cleaning Paint Pads

1 • Squeeze as much paint out of the pad as you can.

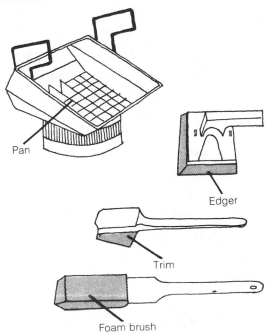

A paint pan and a few of the paint pads found in most hardware stores.

2 • Wash the pad in solvent while squeezing it to get rid of all the paint in the foam rubber.

3 • Rinse with clear solvent.

4 • Squeeze out any excess solvent.

5 • Wrap the pad in heavy paper or foil; store it pad side upward.

Preparing Exterior Surfaces For Paint

WOOD

If you have never had any experience painting wood, accept this fact: The end result of your painting is in direct proportion to how well the wood surface is prepared. Relatively, you should you spend 25% of your time putting on the final coats of paint; the other 75% is dedicated to preparing the surface. There is no particular order for preparing an exterior surface, but all of these things must be done:

Renailing • Hammer in any nails that have popped partially out of the siding. If the nails do not seem to be holding the siding, drive a second nail into the wood about an inch away from the first on the same horizontal plane. That is, nail next to the first nail, not above or below it. Particularly with shakes or shingles, solid sheathing may not be everywhere under the siding. Use rust-resistant siding nails and treat them the same way the existing nails are treated. If the existing nails are countersunk and their heads covered with caulking or wood putty, do the same thing. If the heads of the old nails are showing, you can allow the heads of your new nails to show.

If, during your inspection of the nails, you find traces of rust around any of the nail holes, sand the rust out of the wood or it will show through the finish paint.

Scraping • You must remove all flaking, loose, blistered, or imperfect paint. You can do this with a putty knife, a hooked scraper, or a wire brush. When you are scraping an area, keep working until you reach solid paint that res ists coming off the siding. You do not want any loose paint anywhere on the exterior surface; a fresh coat of paint over loose paint will not adhere, except for the first few days. If you are confronted by a large portion of wall that must be scraped, it may pay to strip the paint using a gel-type chemical stripper, but in most cases this should not be necessary.

Sanding • When the areas of loose paint have been scraped, they will leave sharp ridges of hard paint around their edges that show through the primer and new paint. Sand the ridges so that they feather down to the bare wood, and also give the bared areas a light sanding. Technically, the wood should be sanded with a coarse, then a medium, and finally a fine grade of abrasive paper or steel wool. However, if you have a large number of areas to deal with, you may be able to shorten your working time by using only a medium grit paper. You do not have to do the sanding by hand, however; a disk, vibrating, or belt sander can do the job more quickly for you.

Washing • If you have raw wood anywhere, it should be dusted thoroughly before you paint it. All surfaces that are chalked, faded, or dirty, must also be washed with mild detergent and warm water, and then rinsed off with cold water (you can use a garden hose for your rinsing). Never apply an oil-based or alkyd paint over a damp surface, both will have trouble adhering to the wood. You can apply latex paint on wood that has some moisture in it.

Priming • Use a quality oil-based primer on all raw wood. Any knots in the siding should be coated with shellac and then primed. The shellac prevents resins in the wood from discoloring your finish paint. All exposed metal must be given a rust-resistant primer.

Prime all exposed wood including the insides of any joints that you intend to caulk. When the primer has dried, caulk all open joints.

Caulking • When you have cleaned, scraped, and sanded all of the exterior surfaces to be painted, there is one final chore: caulking (see pages 99–102). Check all seams in the outside of your house and remove any caulking that is loose or badly cracked. Caulking should be firmly embedded wherever dissimilar materials form a joint, such as under thresholds, around water faucets, porch columns, steps, around windows and doors, and along the edges of all trim at the corners of the building. If you elect to use an oil-based caulk, you can apply it to the seams before any primer is put on the house, but most caulkings must be applied over a primer coat.

METAL AND MASONRY

Metal • Any metal surfaces that you intend to paint must be smooth. Scrape or chip off all loose paint and sand the exposed areas, feathering out the hard paint edges. If there is rust on the metal, scrub it off with a wire brush. Wipe away any dust or metal filings and apply a rust-resistant primer under your finish paint.

Masonry • Before you paint any concrete or masonry, clean the surface of all loose particles with a wire brush. Any cracks or holes should be filled (see Chapter 7) and there should be no grease or oil on the surfaces to be painted. You can usually wash oily substances off masonry with a strong detergent.

If the masonry is in such disrepair that a wire brush does not clean it, you may have to sandblast it, an activity that demands some heavy equipment that is best handled by a specialist.

WINDOWS

Windows can take an awesome beating from the weather. The putty around the glass deteriorates, and the sills, which are the exterior counterpart of the interior stools, can develop cracks and rot. Anytime you are painting your house exterior is an excellent time to shore up the windows as well. The first step in renovating a deteriorated window is to clean it of all loose paint and caulking, as well as chip out all loose putty around the panes of glass. The purpose of the putty is to form a watertight seal around the perimeter of the glass. Putty does not hold glass in its frames, the glazier's points underneath it do that, so there is no need to remove the window from its frame. Just stand on your ladder and chip away with a putty knife until you have cleaned

off all of the loose putty around the pane. The grooves in the wood that hold the glass must be cleaned down to the bare wood. Sooner or later you will encounter chunks of putty tough enough to resist a hammer and chisel. When the chisel fails, you have two recourses:

• Apply a propane torch or the tip of a soldering iron to the putty. Wrap tin foil around the soldering iron tip to keep it from being gummed up with putty.

• Chemicals such as paint remover, lacquer thinner, or muriatic acid also soften putty.

Two kinds of putty are used to set glass: Linseed oil putty and glazing compound, which has a latex base. Either will do a satisfactory job. If you are using glazing compound, the grooves in the wooden sash must be primed with paint. If you are using linseed oil putty, first brush the grooves with boiled linseed oil. This step keeps the new putty from drying and cracking prematurely.

Replacing Putty

1 • Remove all loose putty.

2 • Remove all debris from the putty channels.

3 • Paint the exposed wood with boiled linseed oil (or paint).

4 • Press a bead of fresh putty in the joint between the wood and glass.

5 • Smooth the putty with a putty knife, angling it 45°.

Replacing Glass Panes

1 • When you have cleaned the sash of all glass and old putty, measure the sash opening

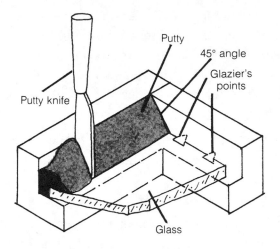

Smooth putty to a 45° angle around a window pane.

and subtract ⅛" from both the length and the width.

2 • When you put glass in the sash, it should not touch wood anywhere. It should float in a bed of putty so that it is sealed against moisture and will not rattle. Spread a $^1/_{16}$" layer of putty on the bottom and side of the grooves, around the sash opening. Push the glass into the grooves and distribute the putty evenly. There must be no gaps in the putty anywhere.

3 • Hammer glazier's points into the wood above the pane. You can use the traditional metal triangles, push points, or plain brads. The metal fasteners should be 8" to 10" apart along each side of the glass.

4 • Make long rolls of putty about ¼" in diameter and press them against the edges of the pane.

5 • Smooth the putty to a bevel by pressing it down with a putty knife drawn along the top of the roll. Your knife blade must be kept clean, so wipe it periodically on a pad

of steel wool moistened with linseed oil.

6 • Paint should be applied only after the putty has dried for at least three or four days, and should extend beyond the putty onto the glass to form a watertight seal. If you stick masking tape to the glass $^1/_{16}$" away from the putty you will be able to paint a straight line on the glass.

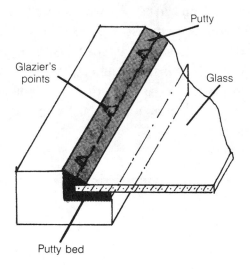

The position of a glass pane in a window sash.

Repairing Window Sills

The sill of a window is the outside bottom horizontal member, which is angled downward so that it can shed water.

There are two ways of renovating window sills so they will shed and not absorb water: with putty and preservative or with plastic wood, depending on the condition of the sill. In both cases, all cracks in the sill must be filled so that you have a smooth surface that slopes away from the house, preventing water from flowing against the window frame. Also check the joints between the sill and vertical rails of the window to be sure they are caulked and painted, preferably with an oil-based paint.

Putty and preservative • If the surface of the sill is intact but has cracks and holes, scrape away all loose paint and debris. Then:

1 • Soak the wood with pentacholorphenol wood preservative.

2 • Wait a day for the preservative to soak into the wood, then saturate the sill with boiled linseed oil.

3 • Fill all cracks and holes with putty.

4 • Wait two days for a skin to form on the putty. Then prime and paint the sill.

Plastic wood • If the sill is badly deterio-

rated and slopes toward the window, it must be built up to a pitch that forces water to roll away from the house.

1 • Mix a paste of fine sawdust and waterproof glue, or use plastic wood to reconstruct that surface so that it slopes away from the window. If you have to build up more than ¼″, apply several layers of material, permitting each to dry thoroughly.

2 • After the final cost has dried, sand, prime, and paint.

Painting the Outside of Your House

PAINT IN DRY WEATHER when the temperature is at least 40°F. The surfaces to be painted must be dry, so wait until the morning dew has evaporated. If it has been raining every day for the past month, wait at least three days before painting; after a day of heavy rain, wait a minimum of a day.

If the siding is new or bared, it requires a coat of primer and then two coats of finish paint. If the surfaces are old but in reasonably good condition, you may get away with a primer and just one coat of finish paint, or the finish paint alone.

Before you paint, cover any concrete or blacktop with newspaper or plastic sheeting and anchor it with stones. Bushes can be covered with plastic drop cloths or newspapers;

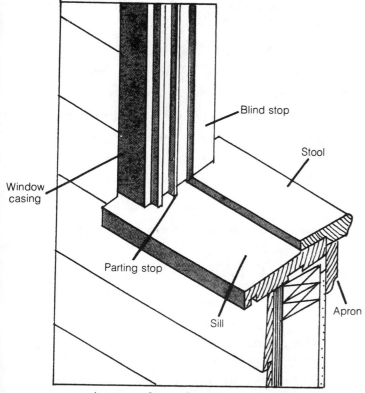

Anatomy of a window sill, stool, and frame.

Blind stop

Stool

Window casing

Parting stop

Sill

Apron

hang newspapers over the tops of screens and doors with masking tape.

Estimating Paint

The labels on most cans of exterior house paint will tell you how much area you can expect the can to cover. As a rule, figure 500 square feet per gallon and 625 square feet for an imperial gallon. To estimate the area you must cover, follow this procedure:

1 • Measure the average height of the walls from the top of the foundation to the eaves. At the gable ends, where the roof is pitched, add 2' to your average height figure.

2 • Measure around the house at the top of the foundation walls to determine the perimeter.

3 • Multiply the average height times the perimeter of the foundation.

4 • Divide by 500 (square feet per gallon). The result is the number of U.S. gallons of paint needed to cover the house.

An average six- to eight-room house will also require one U.S. gallon of trim paint.

Painting Sequence

1 • Begin painting at the top of every surface to be covered. With a house this means starting under the eaves, with the gutters and eaves trim.

2 • Paint the main portions of the house, the shingles, shakes, or siding, first. You should work across the width of the wall, covering the widest horizontal strip possi-

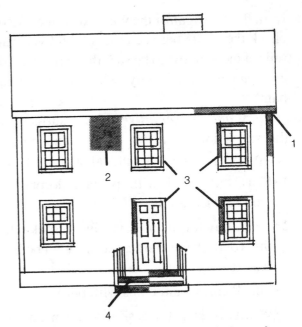

The numbers indicate the order in which the surfaces of the house should be painted.

ble, then continue painting horizontal strips until the whole wall is covered.

3 • Apply the trim paint around all windows, doors, cornices, masonry, and metal.

4 • Paint decks (porches, patios) last.

5 • Because storm windows, screens, and shutters are usually removable, you can save these for a rainy day and do them indoors.

PAINTING LAP SIDING

Clapboard, shingles, and shakes can be painted with brushes, rollers, or paint pads. Paint the bottom edge of lap siding first, covering perhaps four or five courses at a time. Then paint the siding face, always working with the grain of the wood. Once you begin a course, finish it so that lap marks will not show in the paint. Wipe off any drips as soon as they occur.

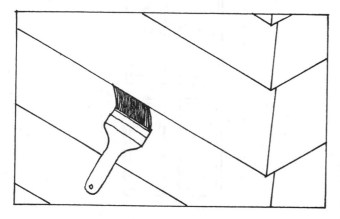

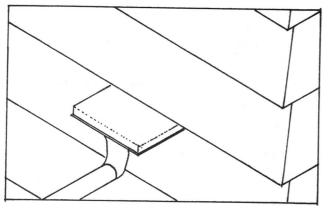

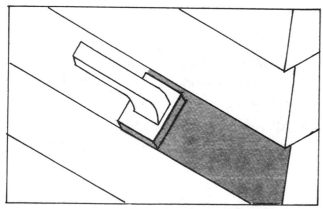

Paint the bottom edge of each board first, then do the face, regardless of what painting tool you are using.

Shakes and shingles • If your shakes or shingles are already painted, all you can do is paint them again to preserve them. If they are presently stained, the stain may bleed through whatever paint you put over it, so test a few inconspicious places to see if the stain shows through your paint. If it does, don't paint them. You can restain them or put on a coat of clear preservative. But if the stain does not show through the paint, paint over the stain, always working vertically.

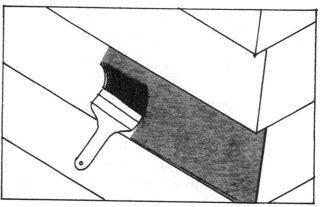

Shingles and shakes are painted vertically, with their grain.

PAINTING DOORS, WINDOWS, AND TRIM

Doors • Doors should be completely painted at one time so that no paint ridges have a chance to form anywhere.

Windows • Sash and trim brushes are designed for painting the narrow parts of window sashes, but so are some rollers and paint pads. Cover the perimeter of the glass with

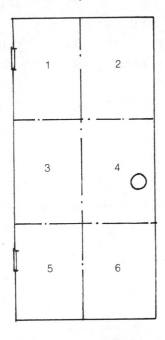

Sequence of painting flush doors.

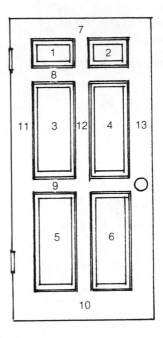

Sequence for painting paneled doors.

masking tape, placed $1/16''$ from the putty, to prevent the paint from getting on the pane. Any paint that does get on the glass can be easily removed by wiping it with a cloth dipped in solvent.

Trim • All of the trim around the doors, windows, and corners of your house must be covered with an oil-based trim paint. You can use brushes, rollers, or paint pads, but the best way of painting the balustrades in porch or step railings, is to use a painting mitten.

Painting Flush Doors

1 • Begin at the top rail and cover the upper lock-side corner.

2 • Do the upper hinge-side corner.

3 • The center of the lock-side.

4 • The hinge side of the center.

5 • The bottom lock-side corners and the rest of the bottom hinge-side.

6 • All edges.

7 • Do the reverse side of the door, following steps 1–5.

Painting Paneled Doors

1 • Cover each panel, starting at the top and working toward the floor.

2 • All horizontal frame members, starting at the top and working down to the bottom rail.

3 • All vertical frame members. Begin at the lock-side edge and work toward the hinged side.

4 • All edges.

5 • Cover the reverse side of the door, following steps 1–3.

Painting Sequence for Casement Windows

1 • Mullions.   4 • Meeting sill.

2 • Crossbars.   5 • Frame.

3 • Cross rails.

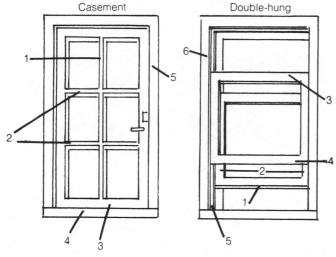

Sequence for painting windows.

Painting Sequence for Double-hung Windows

1 • Meeting rail.

2 • Vertical sash members.

3 • Top edge of the lower sash.

4 • Bottom edge of the lower sash.

5 • Insides of all channels.

6 • Frame.

Allow the paint to dry overnight, then move the sashes before they stick.

PAINTING DECKS

Decks are exterior floors and should be repaired and sanded before any paint is applied to them. Wooden decks are painted with brushes, rollers, or pads, in the same way you paint wood. If you use a roller, first paint around the baseboards and edges with a 3″ brush, then work from the far ends of the deck toward a door or steps. The roller should be rolled lightly over the deck.

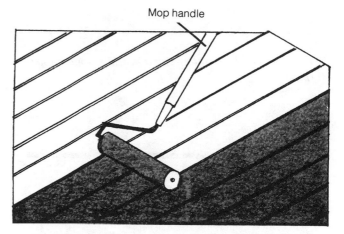

Screw a mop handle into the handle of your paint roller so you don't have to bend over as you are painting a deck.

PAINTING MASONRY

The easiest way to paint brick, concrete, stucco, or cinderblock is with a long-napped roller or a stiff-bristled brush.

Remove all oil and grease from the surface by scrubbing it with a solution of trisodium phosphate (TSP) and hot water or any other strong detergent. Put the paint on liberally, brushing (or rolling) it out in all directions. If you are adding a second coat, give the first application at least 24 hours to dry.

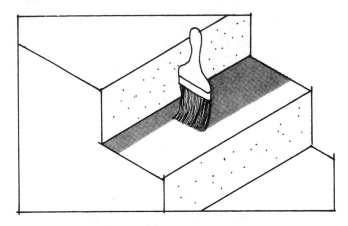

Masonry can be painted with a brush or long-napped roller.

Paint Failures

PAINT PUT ON THE OUTSIDE of a house can fail to produce the desired results for any number of reasons: inferior paint; the wrong paint for the surface covered; improper mixing, the wrong application or priming procedures; moisture getting under the paint.

Blistering • Blisters may occur because of excessive moisture or temperature. *Moisture blisters* come from too much moisture from the house. *Temperature blisters* occur when paint is applied under a direct sun or on a very hot day. To determine what kind of blister you have, puncture the blister. If water comes out it's a moisture blister.

You can prevent blisters: Do not paint on a very hot day or in direct sunlight. You can minimize the amount of moisture coming from your house by installing small vents

below your windows. The vents are ¾"–1"-diameter plugs, which have screens over their openings. To install, drill a hole through the siding that is the same size as the vent and then push the plug into the hole. To get rid of existing blisters, sand or scrape the area, then prime and repaint the bared wood.

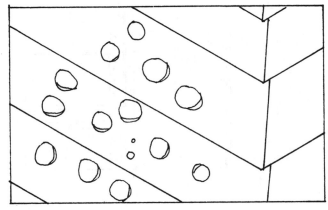

Blisters.

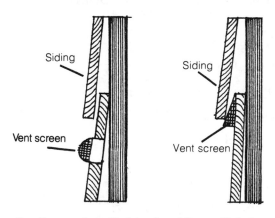

Small vents installed in the siding will help prevent blistering.

Alligatoring • This is when the paint is cracked and wrinkled, resembling alligator skin, and usually it is caused by incompatible paints. Sand the paint off and repaint the area.

If the alligatoring is made up of small cracks, it is called *checking*. It may be possible to cover it with a fresh coat of paint.

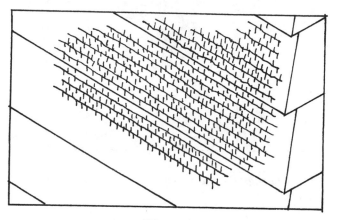

Alligatoring.

Chalking • This occurs when excessive pigment washes out of the paint and becomes a powder. Chalking occurs when you have painted over badly weathered wood that was not properly primed, or if inferior paint was used, or if the paint was put on in cold weather. Wash the chalked areas and repaint.

Crawling • If your paint puddles, it is usually because of a heavy accumulation of dirt. Clean the surface thoroughly, sand lightly, and repaint.

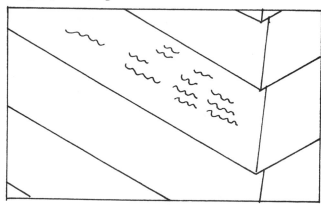

Crawling.

Spotting • When parts of a painted surface lose gloss or color, you probably did not apply enough paint. There is no real answer except to wait until it all blends together.

Cracking (peeling) • This is alligatoring in its advanced stages, and can be remedied by sanding clean and repainting.

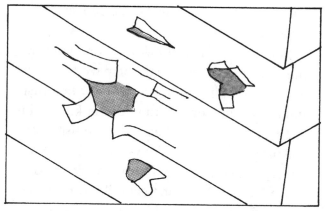

Cracking.

Wrinkling • This looks like wrinkled aluminum foil and comes from applying too much paint. Sand the area down; you may have to repaint it.

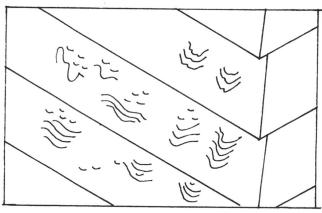

Wrinkling.

Tackiness • This occurs because the oil in the paint may have been slow-drying or the solvent may have been of a poor quality. If you painted in damp weather or on a damp surface, the paint might remain tacky for a long time. If the paint is of good quality, it will eventually dry; if not, it may never dry, in which case remove it and start over again.

Runs and sags • These result from applying too much paint and not brushing it out enough. The runs can be sanded and then repainted.

Stains • Stains from knots or nailheads must be sanded down to the bare wood. Countersink the nails and cover them with a rust-inhibiting putty or caulking. Cover knots with shellac, then a primer, and then a finish paint.

Mildew • Mildew shows up in damp, shaded areas, and it will grow on fresh paint as well as old. You can treat mildew by washing it off with a fungicide, although ordinary chlorine bleach is even more effective.

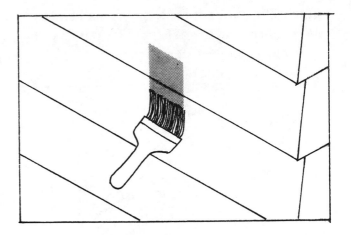

Runs and sags should be wiped off immediately and repainted.

chapter 7

REPAIRS TO MASONRY

Concrete

CONCRETE IS COMPOSED OF portland cement, small aggregate (sand), and large aggregate (gravel, stones), and is used in foundation walls and footings as well as driveways, patios, floors, slabs, and sidewalks. It is one of the cheapest and most durable of all building materials and can be finished in a variety of colors and textures.

If you were mixing cement for a whole project, such as a driveway, you would require a large mixing machine, which can be rented, or you could have your cement delivered to you by a truck already mixed. But if the work at hand is a matter of filling large holes in existing concrete work, you might find it more economical to purchase your cement in 94-pound bags (the only way it is sold), along with the necessary large and small aggregate, and then mix them yourself. For most home repairs, however, you will not need an excessive amount of material, so it is easiest to buy a prepackaged concrete mix in 25-, 40-, or 90-pound bags. These contain all of the dry ingredients in the proper proportions, and all you have to do is mix them with the correct amount of water, as stipulated on the face of the package.

Among the prepackaged cements and concretes offered at your local building supply outlet, you will discover latex and epoxy cements. Both types are more expensive than other cements, but their ability to be feathered out to a thin film makes them excellent for many of the concrete repairs necessary around the home, such as filling small holes and cracks. Your only reason not to consider buying them is cost. They *are* expensive; so for large jobs, their cost makes them prohibitive. Whenever you use a latex or epoxy cement, first clean out the area to be filled with a wire brush, then thoroughly dampen the damaged area. Apply the cement in thin layers until you have built it up to a level with the rest of the concrete.

Estimating Concrete

Portland cement is sold in 94-pound bags, because 94 pounds makes one cubic foot of cement. Both large and small aggregate are sold by the ton or the cubic yard. So to determine how much material you need to fill a given area you must estimate how many cubic feet it measures and then convert that figure to cubic yards:

1 • Measure the length, width, and depth of the area to be concreted. In most cases the length and width will be in feet and the depth in inches.

2 • Multiply the length (in feet) times the width (in feet) times the depth (in inches), and never mind what they told you about mixing apples and oranges in fifth-grade math.

3 • Divide the result of your multiplication by 12 (inches, actually). The result will equal the cubic feet of your area. The formula looks like this:

$$\frac{Length \times width \times depth}{12} = \frac{Cu.\ area}{12} = Cu.\ ft.$$

Mathematically that formula is impossible, but for all practical purposes it works.

However, both sand and gravel are sold by the cubic yard or ton, so you have to convert the cubic feet of the area to be filled by dividing by 27. One cubic yard of concrete requires 6 94-pound bags of portland cement, 1,400 pounds of sand and 2,000 pounds of stone or gravel.

Mixing Concrete

Concrete is heavy and difficult to move, so mix it as close to your site as possible. You do your mixing on a sheet of plywood, any concrete surface, in a wheelbarrow, or anyplace that is flat, hard, and can be hosed clean when you are finished.

1 • Use half a bag of cement at a time and mix it thoroughly with the appropriate amount of sand.

2 • Add your gravel and blend the three ingredients thoroughly. With prepackaged concretes, simply empty the bag and mix the ingredients together with your shovel.

3 • Shovel the cement, sand and gravel into a mound and dig out a hollow in its middle. Fill the hollow with water and blend it into the dry ingredients. Well-mixed concrete will slide off your shovel and be just wet enough to stay together. If the concrete is watery, add more gravel and sand.

REPAIRING CONCRETE

With enough time, cracks and breaks will show up in practically any concrete surface.

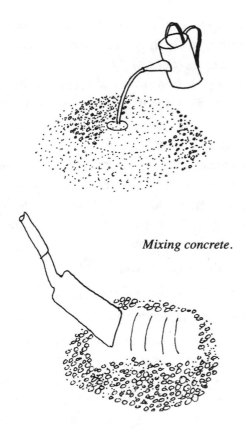

Mixing concrete.

2 • Brush all excess dirt and water out of the crack.

3 • Mix standard portland cement with just enough water to make a thick paste.

4 • Force the cement paste into the crack, using a trowel or putty knife.

5 • Wait about two hours. When the cement paste has begun to harden, cover it with a plastic sheet.

6 • Once a day during the next five days, lift the plastic sheet and sprinkle water on the new cement, so that it will cure properly and not crack again.

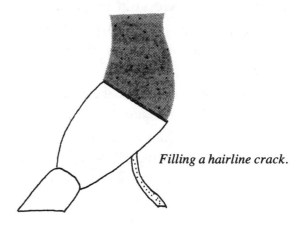

Filling a hairline crack.

They can occur because of settling, weather conditions, or just plain wear, in sidewalks, driveways, walls, stairs, patios, and floors. They begin as hairline splits that are easy to ignore; however, if you ignore these cracks, water will trickle into them and then freeze, and the hairline cracks will get bigger and bigger until they becomes fissures that demand immediate attention. The message in all this is, when you find any kind of crack in concrete work, do something about it as soon as you can.

Filling Hairline Cracks

1 • Moisten the crack and the area around it, and keep it damp for several hours.

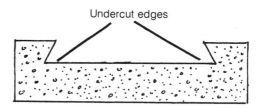

Undercut edges

Cracks more than $1/16''$ wide must be enlarged with a chisel and the edges undercut before filling.

Filling Large Cracks

Any cracks that are over $1/16''$ wide must be chipped out and enlarged with a cold chisel. As you work along the edges of the crack, undercut them so that the base of the repair will be locked beneath the overhang, giving your new cement a better bond.

1 • Widen the crack with a cold chisel and undercut all edges.

2 • Soak the area with water overnight. One way to do this is to let a garden hose trickle water down the crack. An even easier method is to wait for a long rain and do your repair work immediately thereafter.

3 • Clean out all excess dirt and water.

4 • Mix 1 part cement to 3 parts sand with enough water to create a cement that can barely be worked with a trowel.

5 • Trowel your cement into the crack. Level it with the old concrete.

6 • Cure the patch for a minimum of five days.

You can improve the adhesion of new concrete in a crack by mixing enough cement with water to get the consistency of paint and then coating the edges of the cracks with this mixture. Don't let the cement "paint" dry, but apply the new cement immediately.

Surface Blemishes

Scaling, crazing, and dusting can occur in concrete that was not properly placed and should be repaired as soon as they occur.

Scaling • Scaling happens when pieces of concrete flake off a surface, and is the result of improper finishing or of freezing and thawing that took place before the concrete was fully cured.

Crazing • Crazing is a lot of fine cracks on the surface of fresh cement. It happens when concrete dries too rapidly.

Dusting • When a concrete surface breaks into a fine powder it is caused by too much clay or silt in the cement mix, or by improper finishing techniques.

Repairing surface blemishes • If the damage covers a large area and is deep, chip out the entire area and undercut the edges. The following steps hold whether the damaged area is deep or shallow:

1 • Soak the concrete overnight.

2 • Scrub off all dirt and excess water.

3 • Paint the surface with concrete "paint."

4 • Cover the damage with new concrete.

If the damage is deep, use a standard concrete mix with large aggregate; if shallow, a sand-cement-water mix is sufficient. Apply the patch cement in layers about $1/4''$ thick and smooth each layer with your trowel. Let the water sheen evaporate on each layer before you make the next application. Even out and smooth the top layer of concrete, then try to match the texture of the old concrete as best you can.

Repairing Broken Corners

If the corner of a slab or step has broken off in large pieces, you may be able to recement it with latex or epoxy cement. Otherwise rebuild the corner with new cement.

1 • If the corner has crumbled, soak the old concrete.

2 • Clean out all dirt and excess water.

3 • Mix a cement "paint" and cover the damaged area.

4 • Mix a concrete with 1 part portland cement to 3 parts sand and fill in the corner.

5 • After the patch has started to harden you can shape it and work the surface to match the rest of the old concrete.

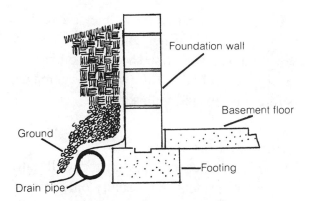

A cross section of a basement seen from underground.

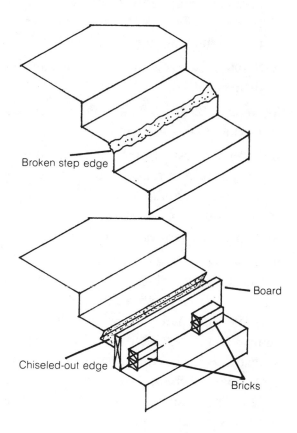

Repairing the crumbling edge of a concrete step.

REPAIRING CELLARS

Water entering a basement can be due to faulty construction, or it might be because the drainage system that should have been installed around the outside base of the founda-tion either does not exist or in some way has failed to function properly. Unfortunately, the only absolute way of drying out a basement entails a tremendous amount of earth moving. All of the soil against the foundation walls of your house must be removed, and while you could do that with your trusty garden spade, you would be doing it for months. So, you have to hire a contractor with a backhoe to do the digging for you (in about a day), but at considerable expense.

Once the walls have been exposed, scrub them clean with wire brushes, then repair any chips or cracks. Then apply a coating of coal-tar pitch to seal and waterproof. The pitch should meet all local building code standards and be painted on the concrete with all brush strokes going in the same direction (horizon-tally, for example). When the pitch has dried, give the walls a second coating, applying the pitch with brush strokes running at right an-gles to the first coat (vertically, for example). You can also plaster overlapping sheets of polyethylene to the pitch for additional pro-tection against moisture.

If you find no drain around the walls, install

drain tile along the base of the foundation, sloping it so that water can run into a storm sewer intake. The drain should be buried in a layer of gravel (1″–1½″ diameter aggregate) before it is covered with soil.

Condensation

Moisture often collects on the walls of a concrete basement, but usually only in summertime. All you can do about it is reduce the moisture content in your cellar with a dehumidifier.

But be sure the problem is condensation and not seepage, by performing this simple test: Tape a bright tin or aluminum sheet to the wall. The metal should be 6″ square and taped at its corners against the concrete. Wait an hour and then examine the metal. If it is moist, you have condensation. If the metal is dry, there is seepage through the walls.

Seepage

Water leaking slowly through cracks in basement walls shows up most often after a rainfall. It may be caused by a poor seal between the walls and floors, or a defective outside drain tile, or the grading may slope toward your house instead of away from it. Occasionally, the drain tiles around the base of the foundation become clogged and overflow. More often the downspouts from your roof gutters are not carrying water far enough from the house. Downspouts work best if they connect to underground pipes that lead to a sewer system or a drywell far enough away from the house to keep the basement from flooding (see pages 56–57).

The seepage you get after a heavy rain can often be corrected with cementitious paints sold as waterproofing agents. These need only have the surface of the concrete dampened before you put them on and they will do a good job, provided the seepage is not severe.

1 • If you have lots of small cracks in your basement walls, mix 1 part cement to 2½ parts damp sand. Add only enough water to make a thick plaster.

2 • Scrub the walls with a wire brush and hose them clean.

3 • Apply a ¼″-thick coat of the cement-sand mixture to the walls.

4 • When the first coat hardens, scratch it with a wire brush to roughen the surface so that the next coat will adhere. Then let the first coat harden for 24 hours.

5 • Apply a second coat, also ¼″ thick.

6 • Spray the wall twice a day for six days.

Cracks larger than ⅛″ wide should be patched separately, with either latex or epoxy concrete. Alternatively, use a mixture of 1 part cement and 3 parts sand mixed to a stiff consistency. Bear in mind that when patching large holes or cracks, you must undercut the edges. Then clean the area, dampen it and force new concrete into the hole, and finish it off flush with the surrounding wall.

Sealing the corner between basement walls and floor • The most frustrating seepage in basements happens along the corner where the floor meets the wall. You may be able to stop the seepage by chiseling out a groove along the floor line and filling it with hot tar.

1 • Begin 1″ or 1½″ above the floor and cut diagonally into the wall and down to the joint.

2 • Pour tar or tar mixed with sand into the

groove. Or use a latex or epoxy cement. The groove surfaces must be damp, but not wet, before they will accept any of the concrete fillers. However, if you are using tar or a tar/sand mix, the concrete must be absolutely dry.

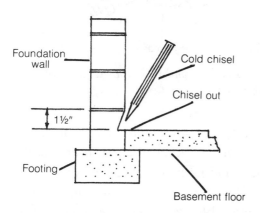

Sealing the corner between basement walls and floor.

STUCCO

Stucco is a concrete. It is made up of portland cement, fine sand, water, and a plasticizer (hydrated lime or asbestos fibers), which make it workable.

Stucco can be applied directly to a rough masonry wall, but on a wooden house it must be anchored to the sheathing by pressing it into a wire mesh nailed to the wall over a water-resistant building paper. If you are adding stucco over plaster, glass block, glazed masonry, or metal, you also have to have the mesh or it will not adhere properly.

Applying Stucco
Stucco is usually applied in three layers, although it is possible to do it with only two applications. The first layer, or scratch coat, is about ½″ thick and is pushed between holes in the mesh. It is then scratched with any tool that will make horizontal lines in its surface. The second, or brown coat, is about ⅜″ and is put on four or five hours after the scratch coat is applied, when some of the moisture has evaporated. This, too, is given a rough surface but is kept wet for two days, so that it can partially cure. The finish coat can have a pigment added to it and can be given any of several textures. It is approximately ⅛″ thick and must be kept damp for five days or so, while it cures.

Repairing Cracks in Stucco
1 • Using a chisel, open the crack until you reach solid stucco.

2 • Undercut the edges of the repair area.

3 • Apply new stucco, packing it into the crack. Wet your repair for at least three days by spraying it two or three times a day.

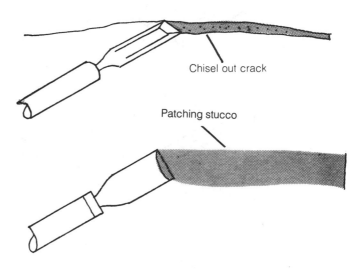

Cracks in stucco should be chiseled out first (top) then filled (bottom).

Patching Stucco

1 • Chisel out all loose or damaged stucco until you can see the mesh.

2 • Clean the area thoroughly.

3 • Undercut the edges of the patch.

4 • Apply a base coat to the patch (if the hole is deep) and cure for five hours before adding the finish coat.

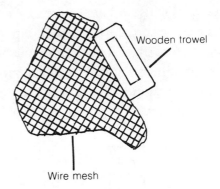

Stucco patches must be allowed to cure before the finish coat is applied.

CONCRETE BLOCKS

Concrete blocks come in all shapes, but are always sized in multiples of 4″. They are made by pouring standard portland cement, sand, and gravel into castings, so for many projects they are an easier way of getting the strength of concrete than to build complicated forms and pour the concrete yourself. There are almost no repairs that can be made to concrete blocks, other than repointing their

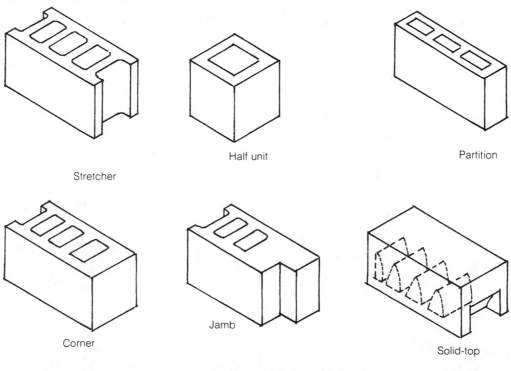

Concrete blocks.

mortar joints or perhaps replacing a broken block.

Mortar • Concrete blocks are held together by bonding them with mortar. Mortar consists of 1 part binder (cement), 3 parts sand, and enough clean water to make the mortar smooth and stiff enough to hold its shape when piled on a trowel. If you are repairing concrete bricks or building a small project, you can purchase premixed mortar in 70-pound bags, which require only that you add water.

Laying Concrete Blocks

Anytime concrete blocks are used to form a wall they must be laid on a footing, which is made by digging an open trench and filling it with concrete. The footing should be twice the width of the wall and placed approximately 18″ below grade. You can make a garden wall as narrow as 4″ thick, if it is not more than 4′ high, but it will be stronger if you make it at least 8″ thick. You do not have to reinforce a concrete block wall that is under 4′ high. Over 4′, you should place ½″-diameter steel support rods in the foundation when it is poured, spacing them every 4′. The rods will stand in the holes in your blocks, which should be filled with concrete when the wall is completed. The wall may continue another 4′ above the tops of the rods and will still be strong.

The secret to laying concrete blocks is to plan your project carefully. Work it out so that your final measurements will be some multiple of 4″, and be certain that the foundation is both square and level. Begin by laying three or four courses of blocks in both directions at

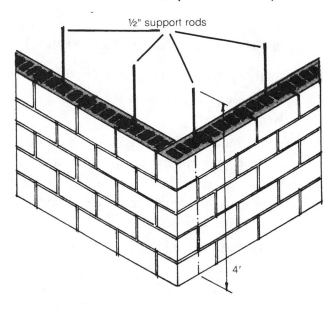

Half-inch support rods must be inserted in any concrete block wall that is to be higher than 4′.

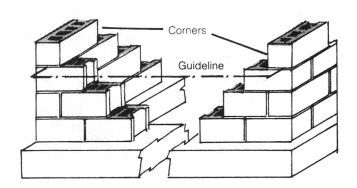

When constructing a wall of concrete blocks, first lay up the corners of the wall, then fill in between them.

each corner. When the corners are in place, stretch a guideline from corner to corner by driving nails into the mortar to act as anchors for the string. The string should just touch the outer edges of the corner blocks so that it becomes a guide for the placement of every block in the course. Then fill in the spaces between corners with more blocks, aligning each block with the string and also leveling it.

How to Apply Mortar

1 • Mix only enough mortar for half an hour's working time.

2 • Apply mortar along the edges on both sides of the cores. The mortar should be applied to the top of the block previously laid, as well as to the bottom and sides of the new block. (Illustration A)

3 • Place the new block firmly against the lower or adjacent block.

4 • Lay a mason's level on the block. Tap the block with the handle of your trowel until it is level and abuts the guide string. (Illustration B)

5 • Scrape off any mortar that squeezes out of the joints and put it on the next block. (Illustration B)

Mortar joints • The average mortar joint should be no more than ⅜″ wide. After you have put the blocks together and scraped off any excess mortar you can make your joints *concave, V-shaped, raked,* or *extruded*. Concave and V joints are normally used in outside work because they shed water; raked and extruded joints are used indoors (they tend to collect water).

How you make the joint depends on the tool you use. The point of your trowel will cut a V joint very nicely. For other joints, a piece of copper tubing does well, but almost anything that will fit into the joint and shape the mortar in the desired manner will do. All you do is pull your tool along the mortar. The action will shape the joint and fill in any voids in the mortar that might allow water to work its way between the blocks.

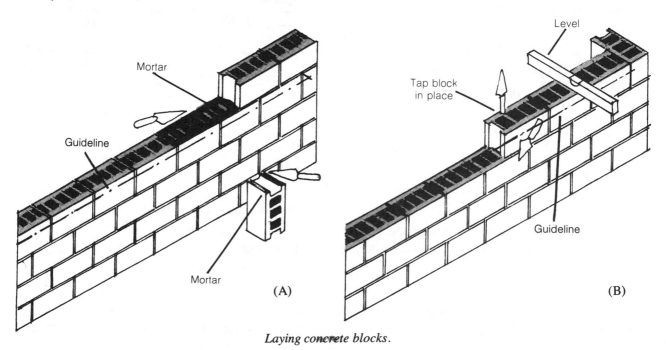

Laying concrete blocks.

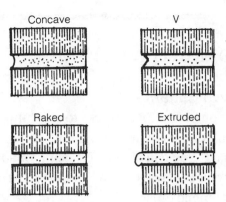

Mortar joints used with concrete blocks.

Bricks

THERE ARE ALL MANNER of bricks made in all kinds of sizes, textures, colors, and grades. The choice of brick for your purpose should be determined by the conditions to which the structure will be subjected when it is completed. For example, *building* (common) bricks are used for wall construction and range from 8″ to 12″ in length. Building bricks are made in three grades: SW (severe weathering), MW (medium weathering) and NW (no weathering). SW bricks can resist freezing, and so are always used in any structure that comes in contact with the ground. MW bricks are more or less frost-resistant, so you can use them in any exterior structure that is above ground level. NW bricks are only for interior work. *Face* brick is made specifically for finished surfaces, and has sharp edges and corners. You can buy it in red, yellow, brown, purple, or black, with either rough or smooth surfaces.

Estimating and Buying Brick

When buying bricks, make sure they are all hard, straight, and the same size. If you pick up any random two bricks and strike them together, they should produce a ringing sound, and will not crumble.

When estimating the number of bricks you need, determine the square footage to be covered and multiply by 7 bricks per square foot. Then add 5% for breakage and waste.

Cement-Lime Mortar

Mortar used with brick can be a dry mix (cement, lime, and sand), to which you add only water, or you can mix 1 part mortar cement (which already contains the right amount of lime), and 3 parts clean sand. If you want to start from scratch, cement-lime mortar requires portland cement, lime, sand, and water. The lime can be either hydrated or quicklime. Quicklime is mixed with water before you add the other ingredients. Hydrated lime is dry-mixed with the portland cement and sand before any water is added. When you are mixing, add water a little at a time until you achieve a mortar that is smooth and uniform in color.

Mortar joints • Mortar joints are finished after the mortar has stiffened, but before it hardens. The mortar is then troweled flush with the face of the brick. In addition to the four mortar joints used with concrete blocks, you can make several other kinds of joints simply by running a jointing tool along the mortar; the jointing tool can be improvised from a piece of pipe or a metal rod.

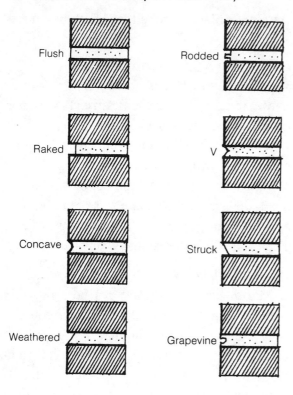

Mortar joints used with brick.

Flush

Rodded

Raked

V

Concave

Struck

Weathered

Grapevine

WORKING WITH BRICK

How to Cut Brick

If you have a lot of bricks to cut, buy or rent a guillotine, which is made for cutting brick by hand. You can also buy masonry blades for your power saws, or you can cut bricks with a hammer and chisel:

To do the latter:

1 • Draw a cutting line with a pencil at the point you want the brick to break away. (Illustration C) Score the brick along the cutting line with a 4″ chisel and a hammer.

2 • Turn the brick over and score the opposite side.

3 • Angle your chisel along the scored cutting line, tilting the handle toward the waste side of the brick. If you strike the chisel

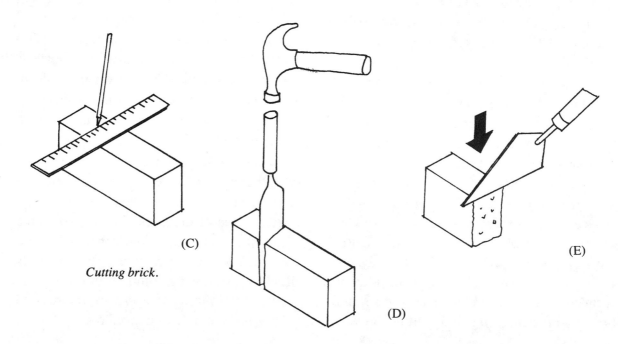

(C)

Cutting brick.

(D)

(E)

sharply, the brick will break cleanly. (Illustration D)

4 • Clean the cut edge of the brick by scraping it with the edge of your trowel or a chisel. (Illustration E)

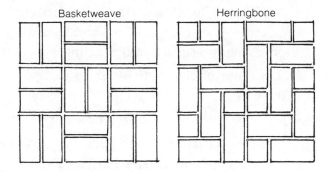

Two of the many patterns for laying bricks in sand.

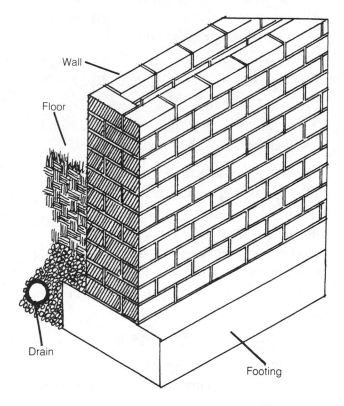

A brick wall and its footings. The drain is optional.

Brick Walls

Brick walls must have concrete or concrete block footings that are at least twice as wide as the wall. The footing must be level and placed below the frost line. Any bricks that touch the footing on or below grade level should be rated SW.

Bricks in Sand

Bricks can be laid in sand to form a patio or walkway without using mortar. Some kind of edging such as wood, concrete, metal, or soldier bricks should surround the project. Soldier bricks can be embedded in concrete and stand vertically, or nearly vertical, around the perimeter of the bricks in sand. Excavate the area to the depth of 3½″. Then fill with sand and level to 1¾″ from ground level. Lay the bricks in the sand bed, abutting them and making them as level as possible.

REPAIRS TO BRICKWORK

Settlement of a brick wall can cause mortar to crumble and cracks to appear in the bricks themselves. Defects in brickwork should be attended to immediately so that water cannot seep into them and cause more damage.

Repointing

Crumbing mortar in the joints will permit water into the wall. If the water freezes and expands, it will cause considerable damage to the wall. So you have to repoint, or tuckpoint, imperfect joints when you find them.

1 • Use a chisel and heavy hammer to chip out any defective mortar. Clean the joint, with

a stiff brush, to at least a depth of ½″, being careful not to chip the bricks. Clean approximately a square yard at a time.

2 • Spray the bricks with water to dampen them.

3 • Mix enough mortar for an hour's work.

4 • Force the mortar into each joint. Fill vertical joints first, then do the horizontals.

5 • Make whatever joint you wish and allow the mortar to harden somewhat, then brush off any waste material.

Filling Cracks in Brickwork

The soil under a brick structure can settle, poor drainage and inadequate waterproofing

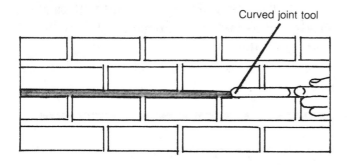

Repointing a mortar joint in a brick wall.

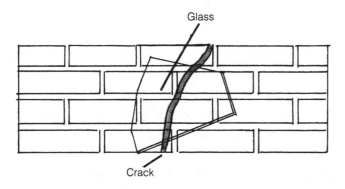

A piece of glass pasted over a crack in a brick wall will break if the structure is still settling.

of a foundation, large tree roots, even rotting wooden members attached to the brick, all can cause cracks in mortar and brick.

When you encounter cracks in brickwork, first find out if the movement of the wall has stopped, by performing either of two tests; in both cases you have to wait several months before you do any patchwork:

1 • Paste a piece of glass over the crack, using epoxy glue. If the structure shifts, it will break the glass.

2 • Fill the crack with plaster of paris. This will also crack if the structure moves.

Repairing Cracks in Mortar • Small cracks in the mortar are usually from improper curing. To repair, chip out the joint with your chisel, then repoint the joint.

Repairing Cracks in Brick • Cracks that run through the brick are hard to fill with mortar, so use grout, and follow this procedure:

1 • Soak the bricks around the crack.

2 • Secure a board over the crack.

3 • Mix portland cement, lime, sand, and water to a runny consistency.

4 • Insert a funnel or a tube as deep into the top of the crack as you can get it.

5 • Pour the grout down the funnel or tube.

6 • Keep the board in place until the grout has begun to harden (at least 24 hours).

Note: You can mix a pigment with the grout to darken it to the color of the brick or existing mortar.

Repairing Cracks Around Door or Window Frames • Cracks around door or window frames occur.because of the expansion and

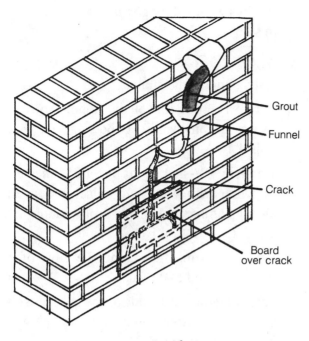

Repairing a crack with grout.

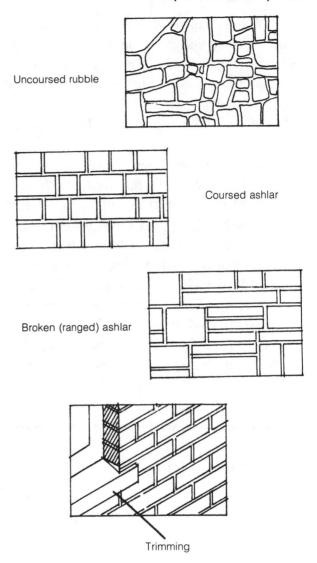

Types of stone construction.

contraction of the wood (caused by changes in weather conditions) against the bricks. To repair these, clean out the crack with your hammer and chisel, then fill the cracks with an elastic caulking compound.

Cleaning Bricks

Keep clean any bricks you are laying by scrubbing them after they are in place. If pieces of mortar are stuck to the brick you can remove them with a solution of 1 part muriatic acid and 9 parts water. Muriatic acid is extremely caustic and must be washed off immediately with water if it gets on your skin. Best to wear rubber gloves when using it. Scrub the solution on the mortar with a stiff brush. Let the acid soak into the brick, then rinse if off with a garden hose. Muriatic acid will also clean the white, powdery stains that appear on bricks.

Stone

GRANITE, SLATE, BLUESTONE, sandstone, marble, and limestone are all used as residence building materials; stonework construction is divided into three classifications:

Rubble construction • This is made up of uncut stones that have no uniform size or shape. They may be put together without mortar in a drywall construction, or it may have mortared joints. Rubble masonry is often used in low retaining walls or foundations.

Ashlar • This involves all of the stones being cut to more or less flat sides, which may be smoothed (dressed) or left rough. If the stones are laid in regular rows, the construction is known as *coursed ashlar;* if there is no continuity to the mortar joints, the construction is called *broken,* or *ranged, ashlar*.

Trimmings • This construction requires the stone be cut, and often dressed, on all sides. Trimmings are used as ornamental details, such as sills, copings, lintels, and moldings.

WORKING WITH STONE

Stone can be cut, split, or drilled. Most stone can be split with a hammer and cold chisel. But if you have trouble, drill a hole to the center of the stone, then insert a stone-splitting tool known as a plug and feather. The feathers are pushed in the hole and the plug is hammered between them.

When you are drilling stone, use a carbide-tipped masonry bit with a power drill. The drill must be rotated at its slowest speed (if it is a multispeed tool), or with a speed reducer attachment (if it is a single-speed unit). Use moderate pressure and drill in short bursts to keep the bit from overheating.

Always wear safety goggles when working with stone.

How to Cut Stone

1 • Fully support the stone.

2 • Scribe a cutting line on the stone. (You can use a masonry nail or the edge of your chisel.)

3 • Hammer a V-shaped groove along the cutting line with your cold chisel and small sledge hammer. Make the groove about ½″ wide. (Illustration F)

4 • Lay the cutting line along the edge of a piece of wood to elevate the stone.

5 • Tap along the waste side of the groove with your small sledge hammer. The stone will break. (Illustration G)

6 • Smooth the ragged edges of the cut with a cold chisel or a sharp, coarse rasp. (Illustration H)

REPAIRING AND REPLACING STONEWORK

Lime- and sand-stones may flake or become pitted and should be treated with chemical preservatives available at building centers. Other small cracks and defects in stone can be repaired with epoxy-based concrete.

Replacing Stone

1 • Use a 4″ bricklayer's chisel to chop out all pieces of the stone.

2 • Clean all loose debris out of the hole.

3 • Cut a new stone to fit in the hole.

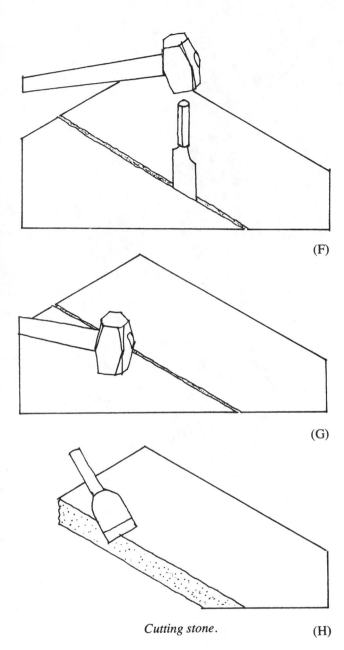

Cutting stone. (H)

4 • Mix 1 part masonry cement with 3 parts sand.

5 • Dampen both the stone and the hole.

6 • Apply mortar to all bonding surfaces.

7 • Put the stone in position.

8 • Repoint the joints.

Replacing Flagstones

Flagstones can be placed in a concrete bed or on sand. When a flagstone in mortar must be replaced, chop out the old stone and clean its cavity of all loose material. If the gravel base under the stone is uneven, tamp it down, level it, then coat it with a layer of mortar. Set the replacement stone in the mortar and fill any voids in the joints with mortar.

Flagstones set on sand must be placed on a bed at least 2″ deep; stones should be at least ½″ apart. When replacing a single stone, fit the stone in place, fill the joints with sand, and level.

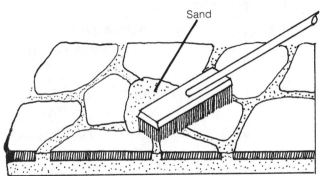

Brush sand into the joints between stones laid in sand.

Blacktop

THE BLACKTOP USED ON most residence driveways is asphalt poured and rolled over a gravel or stone bed. You can purchase a cold asphalt mix at most building supply outlets in 66-pound bags to repair large holes and cracks in the asphalt. Small defects can be filled with an asphalt liquid, which is brushed over the surface.

Repairing Holes in Blacktop

1 • Remove all loose dirt, stones, and crumbling blacktop from the damaged area. You have to keep pulling out debris until the edges around the damaged area are absolutely solid.

2 • Fill all but the last 2″ of the hole or crack with gravel, and tamp it down until it is well packed.

3 • Fill the hole with a 1″-thick layer of the cold asphalt mix. Chop up the mix with a shovel to get rid of air pockets.

4 • Tamp the asphalt until it is packed against the edges of the area.

5 • Fill the patch with enough asphalt mix to mound it ½″ above the surrounding surface.

6 • Tamp the top layer of asphalt material until it is flush with the old blacktop. Driving your car back and forth over the patch does a fine job of tamping it down.

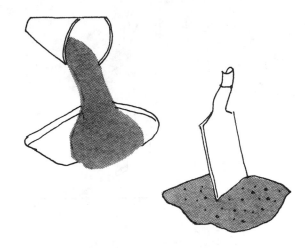

Filling a hole in an asphalt driveway.

chapter 8

FROM PORCHES TO POSTS

CONCOMITANT TO PRACTICALLY every home are likely to be a number of structures that can develop problems. Fences, for example, can become less than sturdy just from standing out in the weather for years on end. Porches can sag, stoops become hazardous, or at best, unsightly. Fence posts loosen; gates resist being opened. With most, but not all of these situations, you are dealing with wood, which, unless it has been preserved against the ravages of nature, may have weakened, although where and how may not be immediately evident when you look at it.

Porches and Stoops

A STOOP IS ESSENTIALLY a small porch. Both are likely to include a step or steps leading up to a wooden deck that is held above grade level by a system of piers and joists; if you were to build solid walls around either a porch or a stoop, you would have a standard room with a crawl space underneath. The maladies that can befall either a porch or a stoop essentially occur from rot getting at one or more of the wooden members used to form the construction. The preventive maintenance, of course, is to protect the structure regularly with either a wood preservative, some form of varnish, or paint.

Fixing Steps

The steps leading up to most porches and stoops are open stringer stairways. The stringers on either side of the steps are notched with a series of L-shaped cutouts, to

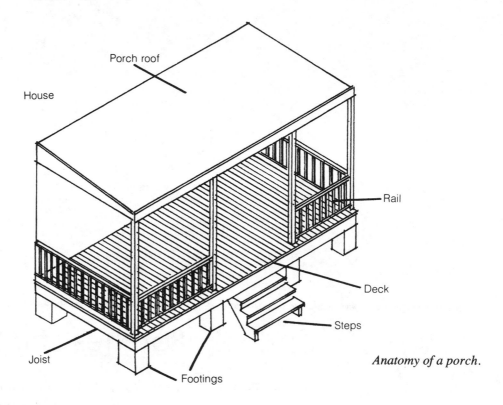

Anatomy of a porch.

the edges of which the treads and risers that form each step are nailed. When any of the steps are broken or badly worn, you can almost always pry them up from the stringers that hold them, measure and cut a new board or boards, and then nail them in place.

You can, in fact, replace the entire stairway without too much trouble. Many lumber yards sell stair stringers, which are already notched, as well as tread lumber, which has been milled to a curve along one edge. All you have to do is cut it into the proper lengths and nail it to the stringers. If you are replacing an entire stairway, use the old pieces as a cutting pattern for your new lumber, then coat the new pieces with a good preservative on all sides and edges. Moisture can creep into any unpro-

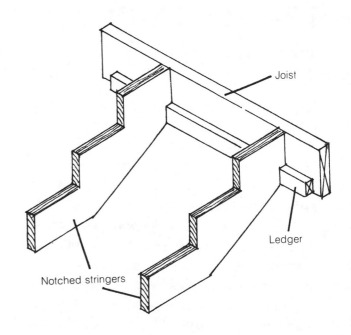

Open step stringers.

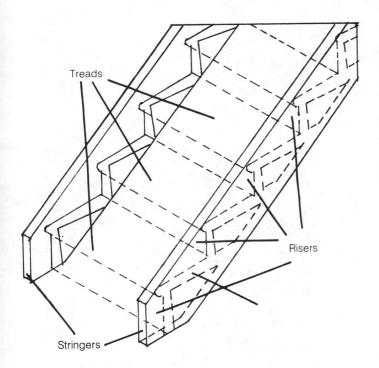

Treads

Risers

Stringers

Many lumber yards sell milled tread lumber which has one edge already curved.

tected centimeter of wood. It can even get into the joints between pieces, and once there it begins to eat away at the wood and eventually rots it. Once you have thoroughly covered every wooden piece with a preservative, you can assemble the pieces and paint or stain them.

REPAIRS TO ROOFED DECKS

If the decks of porches and stoops were indoors, they would be called floors, and they are constructed in exactly the same manner. If you were to crawl underneath your porch you would see regularly spaced piers made of masonry, or merely large posts sunk in the ground, which support a series of joists that run at right angles under the deck. Usually this means the joists are parallel to the wall of the house, so that the deck planks extend at right angles across the narrow width of the porch or stoop. The planking is nailed to the joists and probably runs under the pillars and railings that support the roof over the deck. While the construction is simple enough, all kinds of problems can arise with a roofed deck. The roof can sag, and so can the deck. The railings can rot and become unsafe. The pillars can develop rot, particularly around their base, and massive as they may be, become a hazard.

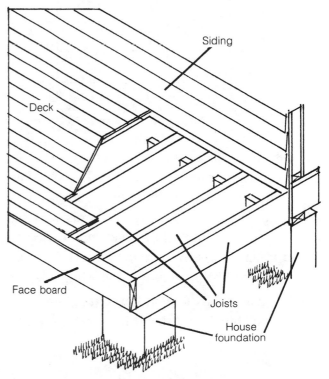

Siding

Deck

Face board

Joists

House foundation

Anatomy of a porch deck.

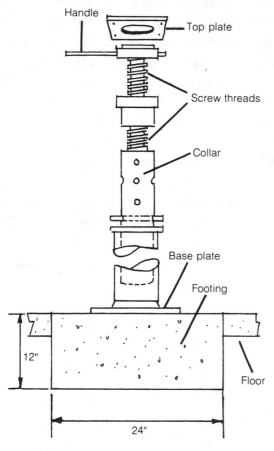

Handle

Top plate

Screw threads

Collar

Base plate

Footing

12"

24"

Floor

A short house jack.

Leveling Porch Roofs

A sagging roof suggests the deck may have developed a slope of its own. If this is not the case, then the roof may not be as well supported as it ought to be and might need additional pillars. Assuming that only the roof is lopsided, the procedure for leveling it is this:

1 • Rent or buy a short house jack. Stand the jack on a 2 × 4 that is long enough to span four or more joists when it is placed on the deck.

2 • Cut a piece of 2 × 4 that can stand in the jack and will be 1½″ shorter than the roof.

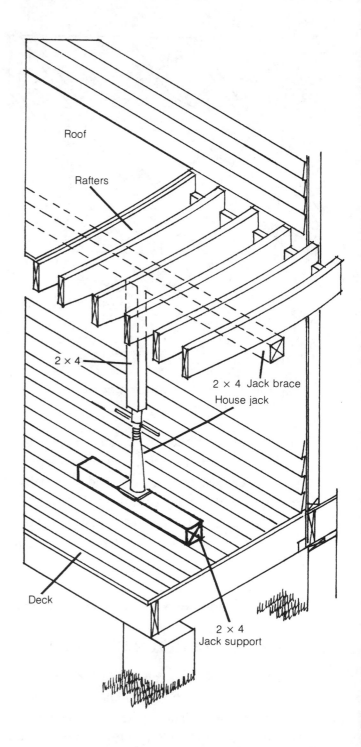

Roof

Rafters

2 × 4

2 × 4 Jack brace

House jack

Deck

2 × 4
Jack support

Positioning a house jack to lift the porch roof.

3 • Nail a long piece of 2 × 4 across the top of the vertical member to span as much of the underside of the roof as possible. Then insert your 2 × 4 T in the jack.

4 • *Very slowly* crank up the house jack. As you push the roof up, you are asking a myriad of timbers to shift their position, which they will do, but grudgingly. If you hurry the process, you will begin hearing the wood crack. If this happens, stop. Wait 24 hours, and then turn the jack no more than one full turn. Then wait another 24 hours before rotating the jack another full turn. You can crank the jack one full turn every day until the roof is as level as you want it to be.

5 • When the roof is level, the jack will hold it in place while you figure out how to support the roof in the manner in which you want it to become accustomed. You may have to nail blocks of wood between it and the tops of the pillars that hold it, or you may need to replace the pillars altogether, or add more pillars.

Replacing Pillars

If a pillar is too short to hold your porch roof level, or if it has become so rotted that it must be replaced, your immediate problem is to find a replacement that is identical with the pillars that will remain under the roof. Large lumber yards often carry pillars in stock, or they can order one or more for you. Best you have the replacement on hand before removing the old pillar.

1 • If the pillar you are exchanging is in the middle of the porch, you may be able to get away with just taking it out and shoving a new one in its place. If the pillar is at a corner or there is no other support for several feet, be a little more wary about pulling it down without first supporting the roof.

The safest approach is to jack up the roof about half an inch with a short house jack and hold it there. By lifting the roof you will take the weight off the top of the old pillar and make it easier to pull it out of its position while the roof is still supported.

2 • When the old pillar is removed, clean the flooring and underside of the roof of all loose dirt and debris, than stand the new pillar in place.

3 • Be certain the new pillar is properly positioned before releasing the house jack, allowing the roof to settle down on the pillar and hold it in place.

4 • Nail the new pillar in place or secure it in the same manner as the old pillar.

You can replace or remove and repair all of the pillars holding up your porch roof, but do them one at a time.

Leveling Sloping Decks

When not only the roof of a porch, but its deck as well, have gotten off level, the cause is most likely settlement of the supports under the deck. If the structure is only slightly off level, the easiest remedy may be to shore up the boards in the deck. If you are faced with a steep slope, then the entire structure must be jacked up until it is level.

1 • Place as many short house jacks as you need under the lowest points in your porch.

One jack can crank up an entire house, but if the porch goes around a corner, you may need jacks at the ends, the outside edges, or at the corner. Each jack must be placed on a broad-based footing made of heavy timbers placed on the ground under the porch. The vertical timber placed in the jack should form a T with a timber that is long enough to span as many of the joists as possible.

2 • When the jacks are in position, crank them up until they become hard to turn, and then stop.

3 • You are in the process of shifting all framing members of both the deck and the roof above it, as well as the pillars, decking, roof sheathing, and roofing materials. That is a considerable number of joints that must realign themselves, so change their positions very slowly. Every 24 hours, tighten your house jacks no more than one-quarter turn.

4 • When the porch is level, insert shims (wooden blocks, bricks, or stones) between the joists and the piers that support them, then release the house jacks.

Replacing Floorboards in a Deck

Often only the edge of a porch or stoop, where the weather has constantly gotten at the decking, needs to be replaced. Years of weathering can rot out the ends of any wood, particularly if it has not been properly painted every two years or so.

If you are replacing part of a board here and there, you must begin by removing the defective member.

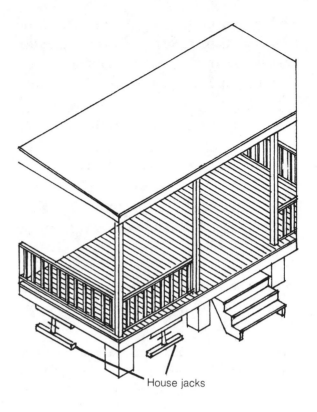

Leveling a deck with house jacks.

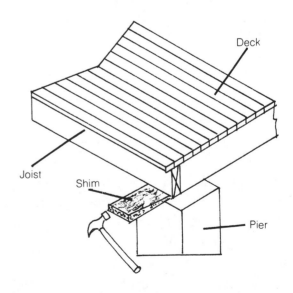

Shims support a once-sagging deck.

The boards that form a deck are nailed to joists that run at right angles to them and are probably spaced every 16″ on center. You can tell where the joists are by locating the rows of nailheads that run parallel to the house wall. Normally, one or two nails are placed in each board as it crosses each joist.

1 • Pry the defective board loose from its joists, using a claw hammer or crowbar. If the entire board is to be removed, you may not be able to lift it any higher than the bottom rung of the railing (2″ – 3″), so you will have to pull out all of the nails that hold it to the joists. Even when the nails are removed, the house end of the board may be wedged under the house siding (where it

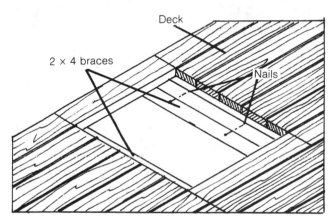

Replacing part of a porch floorboard.

was also nailed). Try pulling the board straight out. If that fails, cut or break it into pieces.

2 • If you are replacing only part of the board, it has to be cut somewhere over the center of a joist. You can do this in two ways. If you have a circular saw, set the blade depth to no more than the thickness of the decking. Remove the nails in the joist and center the saw over the middle of the joist. Lower the blade into the board. The problem with cutting deck boards this way is that your saw blade will probably extend

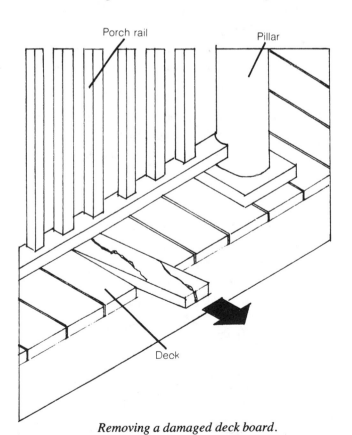

Removing a damaged deck board.

into the boards on either side of the one you are cutting, so it may be neater if you use a saber saw instead.

To cut off an isolated plank with a saber saw, you cannot cut it over the joist, so make your cut not more than an inch in front of the joist. You may also have to drill a hole in the board to get the saw blade through the wood. But at least you will not be in danger of cutting the planking on either side of the defective board.

3 • When the board has been removed, cut a replacement board to fit in the hole. The new board must be nailed to each of the joists it crosses, and at each end. If you have cut the old board over the center of a joist, you will have about ¾″ at the edge of the joist into which you can drive nails. If you cut off the old board with a saber or hand saw, nail a short length of 2 × 4 against the side of the joist, under the severed board. If your cut was no more than 1″ in front of the joist, you will have ½″ of the 2 × 4 to support the end of the new plank and to which to nail it.

Replacing Half a Deck

If all or most of the front portion of a deck needs to be replaced, the job is actually simpler than fixing a few random planks.

1 • Select a joist that is far enough back from the edge of the porch to include all or most of the damaged wood in the deck. Locate the edge of the joist that is farthest from the house wall. If the decking has spaces between the boards, you can follow the edge of the joist just by peering down between the boards. Otherwise you may have to

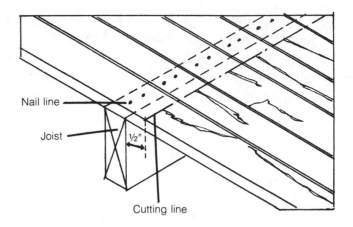

Preparing to remove the damaged portion of a deck.

determine the edge by going under the porch to see where the joist goes. When you know where the edge of the joist is running, draw a cutting line on the deck about ½″ away from the joist and just beyond the nail line. Then drive the nails holding the boards to the joist at both ends up through the deck, and remove them.

2 • Set the blade of your circular saw to a depth equal to the thickness of the decking. There will be cross bracings somewhere along the joist and you do not want to cut into them as you saw the deck, so do not use the saw

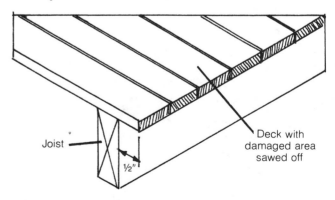

The damaged deck section is removed.

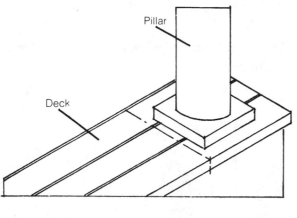

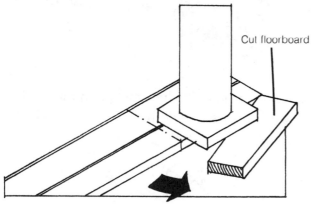

Removing a board from under a porch pillar.

4 • Clean off the tops of the exposed joists. Get rid of all nails and debris.

5 • The old decking should extend ½″ beyond the edge of the joist that you cut along. Nail a 2 × 4 against the joist, making sure that its top edge is forced snugly up against the underside of the planks' ½″ overhang. The 2 × 4 should run the entire length of the exposed joist. You can end it at whatever point the old decking remains. Also nail pieces of 2 ×4 around the base of the pillars if you are not pulling the planks out from under them, and put them anywhere else your new boards will need a support.

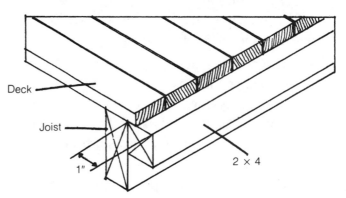

A 2 ×4 nailed to the underside of the deck overhang will support the new boards.

blade at its full depth. Saw along your cutting line.

3 • Pry off each of the boards you have cut. When you reach boards that run under the porch pillars you may be able to pull them out or you will have to saw them off flush with the base of the pillar. If you can pull them out from under the pillars, don't. At least don't until you are ready to replace them with new boards, or the roof is liable to collapse. You can cut them off short, however, leaving just enough of each board to get hold of later.

6 • Cut your new boards to length and position them over the joists. Drive a nail through each board at both ends as well as wherever it crosses a joist.

7 • If you intend to remove the boards under the pillars, do it one board at a time. Pull the first board and immediately insert its replacement, to hold the pillar in place. Then remove the other boards one at a time and replace them.

8 • Prime and paint the new wood as soon as possible after it has been laid.

Fences

MASONRY WALLS ARE BUILT on foundations buried in the ground and rarely develop any major problems (see Chapter 7 for repairs). Wooden and metal fences, however, can become troublesome from rot or rust. The best way to prevent this from happening is to lay your fence posts properly in the first place.

Setting Fence Posts

The proper way of setting a fence post, whether it is metal or wood is:

1 • Dig a hole to a depth equal to one-third of the length of the post. The best tool to use is a post hole digger. The hole should flare at its bottom and be only slightly larger than the post at its top; try to disturb the surrounding earth as little as possible.

2 • Paint the post with a preservative such as creosote or pentachlorophenol (penta). If you stand the post in a bucket of preservative overnight, the liquid will have a chance

Post hole digger.

to thoroughly soak into the end grain of the wood.

3 • Place a flat stone or a shovelful of gravel in the bottom of the post hole.

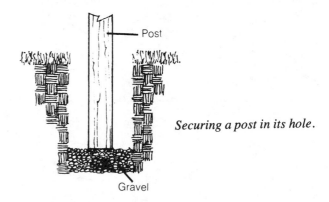

Securing a post in its hole.

4 • Set the post in the hole and plumb it. Nail wood braces to hold it in its vertical position.

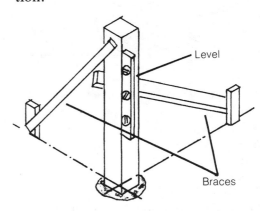

Keep the post vertical with wooden braces.

5 • As a rule, the hole should be filled with concrete tamped tightly around the base of the post. Slope the top of the concrete away from the post so that it can shed water. If you do not slope the concrete, the post is almost guaranteed to rot at its base and collapse within a few years. If the soil is hard, you can often just fill in the hole with well-compacted soil.

6 • Remove the braces after the concrete has hardened.

REPAIRS TO FENCE POSTS

The weakest part of a fence post is at the point where it emerges from the earth. Water runs down the post and collects around its base, where it seeps between the post and the concrete, and sooner or later the wood begins to rot or the pipe rusts. Sometimes the fence shifts and posts begin to wobble in their holes, or, if the post footing was not buried sufficiently below the frost line, it may heave from frost action.

Loose Posts

You can temporarily strengthen a loose post by driving wooden wedges into the hole around the post base. The wedges must be treated with a preservative and, when they are in place, wrapped to the post with baling wire.

If the post was set in concrete and it has heaved because of frost action, remove it from the ground and deepen the hole so that the bottom of the post, when reset, is well below the frost line. In most parts of the United States, the frost line is 6″ or so below ground, but it can be as deep as 1½′. Check your local building code for the exact depth.

Broken Wooden Posts

Wooden posts that have rotted and broken off below grade level can often be salvaged by driving boards or stakes treated with a

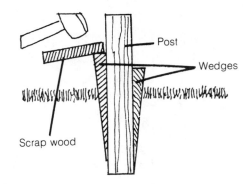

Wooden wedges temporarily strengthen a loose fence post.

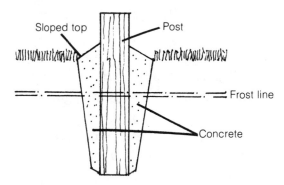

To prevent a post from lifting from its concrete bed, set it well below the frost line.

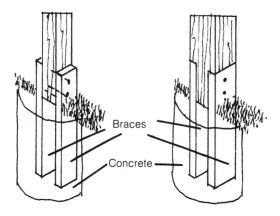

Repairing a post broken off below ground.

preservative into the sides of the post hole and then nailing or screwing them to the post.

If the post was broken off above ground

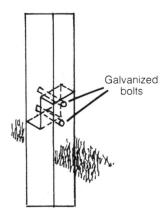

Repairing a post broken off above ground.

level, you may be able to cut notches in the two parts and reassemble them with a lap joint held together with non-rusting (galvanized) bolts.

Posts that break off at ground level present a slightly more complicated repair:

1 • Chisel out the decayed wood left inside the post hole, until you have dug at least 4″ below the top of the concrete. (Illustration A)

2 • Cut out all of the rotted wood at the bottom of the post. Hopefully, there will still be a solid core at the center of the post. If there is not, you can splice a section of new wood to the post and bolt the splice together.

3 • Build a wooden form around the base hole. The form should be set at least 2″ back from the post hole and be about 6″ high. (Illustration B)

4 • Drive nails into the sides of the bottom of the post to give the concrete something it can grip, stand the post in its hole, plumb it, and hold it in place with braces. (Illustration B)

5 • Fill your form with concrete and slope it upward against the sides of the post. (Illustration C)

6 • Remove the forms when the concrete has cured (in about a week).

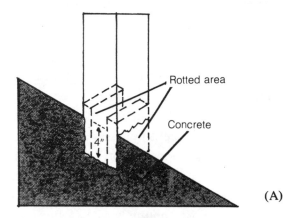

(A)

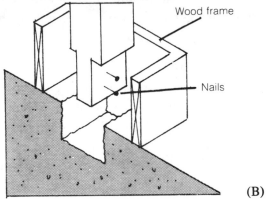

(B)

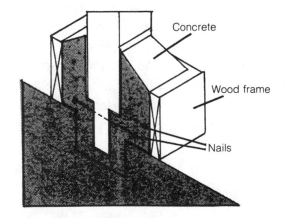

Repairing a post broken at ground level.

Broken Metal Posts

Metal posts can rust and break in much the same way wooden ones rot. It takes a few years more of neglect, but the end result is the same. The posts, of course, can be preserved indefinitely by painting them with a rust-resistant metal paint every few years.

When a pipe-type post breaks off, saw off the rusted area at its base, leaving as much of the pipe as possible above grade level. Then replace the remainder of the post with a pipe that is either just large enough to fit *over* the old pipe or just small enough to slide inside it. Drill holes through the connected pipes and lock them together with a machine bolt.

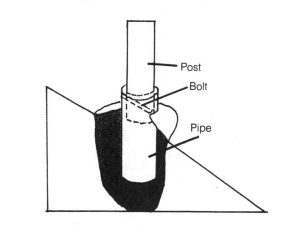

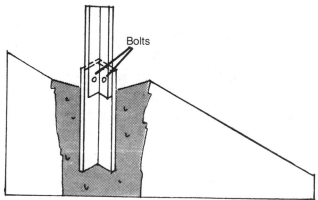

Repairing metal posts. Pipe (top); angle iron (bottom).

If the post is an angle-iron type and it has broken, cut it off, leaving as much of the base above ground as possible, then stand a new angle-iron post next to the stub and bolt the two sections together.

REPAIRING AND REPLACING FENCE RAILS

There are numerous types of fences, from metal mesh and barbed wire to split rail, board, and picket. Nearly every version you encounter will consist of posts that support horizontal rails, which in turn hold vertical, or nearly vertical, members in place. The vertical members, such as the pickets in a picket fence, may rot and require replacement, or they may come loose as the changing weather swells and shrinks the wood around their nail holes. The vertical members of a fence can often be resecured merely by renailing them to the rails. On occasion, such as when rot has gotten into too much of the wood, they may have to be completely replaced. If that's the case, use the old pieces as forms for shaping the new wood.

The rails in a fence, because they are horizontal, do not shed water as readily as the vertical members. Water can, and does, sit on top of the rails, and given enough time and lack of annual maintenance, will rot them. At which point the rails must be replaced. The ends of the rails normally rot first, because the grain is more open to allowing water into the member. The best repair that can be made to a defective rail is to replace it altogether.

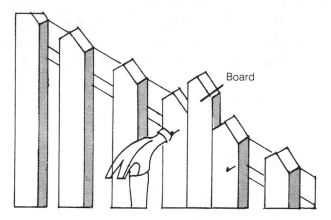

One way to achieve even spacing between pickets is to place a board between them as you nail them to the rails.

Replacement of a rail section can be done between posts, but the repair procedure depends on how the rail is attached. In general, the procedure for replacing rails follows these steps:

1 • Remove the vertical members attached to the rail.

2 • Remove the section of the rail by freeing it at the posts. You will probably have to saw it at each end. (Illustration D)

3 • Cut a new section of rail using the old rail as a guide. You may have to notch the ends, or do whatever is necessary to attach the rail to the posts.

4 • Install the rail between the posts. This may entail nailing, screwing, drilling for bolts through the members, attaching angle irons, or what have you. (Illustration E) But, however the rail and posts are connected, there will be a joint of some kind. Seal that joint with a caulking compound. (Illustration F) In fact, sealing all of the rail-post joints in a fence with caulking will help to prevent rotting.

5 • Coat the new rail with a preservative, and be especially liberal along its top edge, where water will tend to collect and remain for long periods of time.

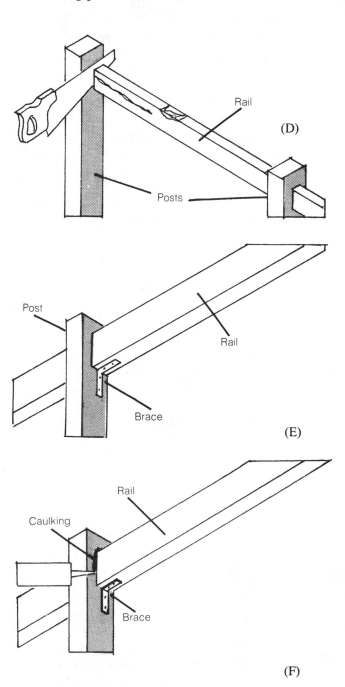

Replacing a section of fence railing.

REPAIRING GATES

Like the fences they are installed in, gates can be of almost any design, but they all will be attached to a post by hinges of some sort. A gate post, standing out in the weather year after year, supporting the weight of a swinging gate, which pulls and leans on it endlessly, is likely to be the first area of repair. The gate can sag from its own weight or pull the post to which it is attached loose in its hole. There are three areas of repair to examine when something goes wrong with a gate: the hinges, post (see pages 149–151), and gate frame.

Gate Hinges

The hinges on a gate are repaired the same way you repair the hinges on any door (which is all a gate really is). However, the special problem with gate hinges is that the wood they are secured to may have rotted so much it can no longer hold the screws. There are three things you can do about loose gate hinges:

- Reposition them so that the screws are in solid wood.

- Remove the hinges and fill the screws holes with wooden plugs coated with a waterproof glue. When the glue has dried, replace the hinges, driving the screws into the plugs. (Illustration G)

- Use longer screws or drill through the gate and hold the hinges in place with bolts. (Illustration H)

Gate Frames

Basically, a gate is nothing more than a frame and panel construction similar to many

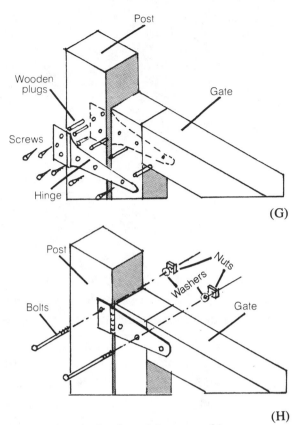

Two methods of repairing a gate hinge.

doors. If there is no solid panel inside the frame, or if the frame supports a series of boards, it is weaker than a door. Moreover, because a gate is outdoors and constantly buffeted by the hot and cold, dry and wet of the weather, it is subjected to coming loose at its joints, as water eventually seeps between the wood and begins to rot it. If the gate has been neglected for too long, it may have to be replaced in part or totally. If the members are loose, but not completely rotted, there are several ways you may be able to extend the life of the gate for a few more years:

- Loose joints between the vertical and horizontal rails can often be taken apart and coated with a waterproof glue.

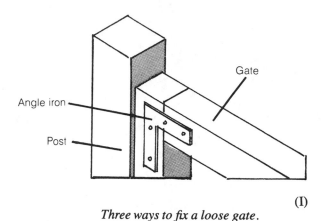

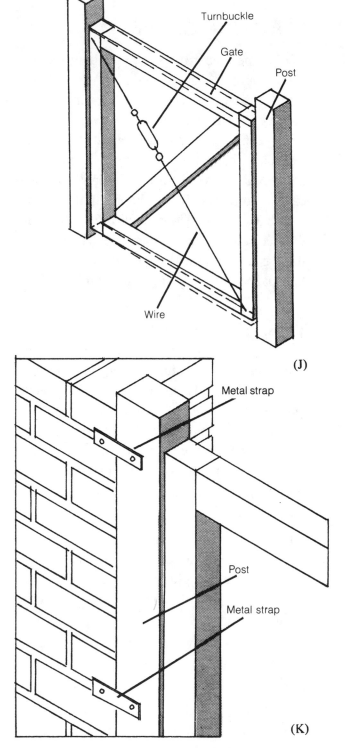

Three ways to fix a loose gate. (I)

- Angle irons or mending straps can be screwed or bolted across the joints between members to stabilize weak unions. (Illustration I)

- A sagging gate may be stabilized by adding diagonal support members. You might use metal, wood, or a wire and turnbuckle. In some ways, the wire and turnbuckle is the most effective, since the wire can be tightened (by turning the turnbuckle) until it holds the gate in exactly the correct position to allow its opening and closing properly. (Illustration J)

- If the post that holds the gate is attached (or just standing against) masonrywork, such as a brick or concrete wall, and the post is wobbly or weak, it can be held to the masonrywork with metal straps screwed or bolted to the wood and secured to the masonrywork with masonry nails or lead plugs and screws. (Illustration K)

INDEX